EVER ANCIENT, EVER NEW

Ever Ancient
EVER NEW

WHY YOUNGER GENERATIONS ARE EMBRACING TRADITIONAL CATHOLICISM

EDITED BY

DAVID DASHIELL

TAN Books
Gastonia, North Carolina

Cover design by Caroline Green

Cover image: "Rorate Mass" of the Blessed Virgin, Advent 2019 © Institute of Christ the King, St. Francis de Sales Oratory, St. Louis, MO. Used with permission. A "Rorate Mass" is the name for a votive Mass of the Blessed Virgin in Advent. It is a tradition for this Mass to be celebrated before sunrise, accompanied only by candle light. Visit: www.institute-christ-king.org

Library of Congress Control Number: 2021946908

ISBN: 978-1-5051-1872-8
Kindle ISBN: 978-1-5051-1873-5
ePUB ISBN: 978-1-5051-1874-2

Published in the United States by
TAN Books
PO Box 269
Gastonia, NC 28053
www.TANBooks.com

Printed in the United States of America

"The great movement of apostasy being organized in every country for the establishment of a One-World Church which shall have neither dogmas, nor hierarchy, neither discipline for the mind, nor curb for the passions, and which, under the pretext of freedom and human dignity, would bring back to the world (if such a Church could overcome) the reign of legalized cunning and force, and the oppression of the weak, and of all those who toil and suffer . . . . Indeed, the true friends of the people are neither revolutionaries, nor innovators: they are traditionalists."[1]

—Pope Saint Pius X

---

[1] Pius X, Encyclical *Notre Charge Apostolique*, 1910.

CONTENTS

PUBLISHER'S NOTE

FOREWORD

"And I will go in to the altar of God: to
God who giveth joy to my youth."
—Psalm 42:4

THIS PRAYER is featured in the opening prayers of the Traditional Latin Mass, which are known as the prayers at the foot of the altar. This prayer perfectly describes the thesis of this book: God, when properly worshiped, brings authentic joy and satisfaction to our youth. It should come as no surprise, then, that younger generations are turning toward the traditional Mass in droves.

Before we discuss the recent trend of younger generations embracing traditional Catholicism, it is important to understand what is meant by the word *traditionalist*. Even though a traditionalist typically adheres to set doctrines or practices, this term is often misunderstood and is therefore highly divisive. Perhaps this is due to the wide spectrum of traditionalists you may have encountered in person or while browsing the internet—some pleasant, and others unpleasant. There are "glad-trads" who are virtuous and friendly and devoted to the traditional liturgy—that is, Holy Mass celebrated exclusively in Latin with the priest facing east. On the other hand, there are the "mad-trads" who take out their anger at liturgical abuse on hapless old women in internet comment boxes. Unfortunately, countless individuals in the Church judge every traditionalist they meet based on the one or two unfortunate encounters they might have had with a mad-trad. As Patrick Archbold wrote in *The Remnant*, these individuals are just as judgmental toward others as the group they are labelling as supposed bigots. He wrote, "They label them as judgmental, holier-than-thou, Pelagian, Promethean, haters of mercy and all the proof required is some comment by some guy in some com box somewhere that was over-the-top and rude. So, [if you are a traditionalist,] you are just like that guy."[1]

There is no shortage of Catholics who are quick to follow the above-mentioned line of reasoning. While it might be true that there are plenty of so called mad-trads who lack charity in internet comment boxes, to judge *every person* who attends the Latin Mass based on a *few* bad encounters you have had is the definition of prejudice. Of course, it does not help when our own Holy Father labels young priests who prefer the traditional devotions of our Faith as rigid, mentally imbalanced, and obsessed with sex.[2] These insults and broad generalizations could not be further from the truth. Traditionalist Catholics love the Church and the pope, and they will

1   Patrick Archbold, "The Most Radical of Traditionalists," *The Remnant*, September 28, 2016, https://remnantnewspaper.com/web/index.php/articles/item/2784-the-most-radical-of-traditionalists.

2   Dorothy Cummings McLean, "Pope Criticizes Young Traditional Priests' Clothes: Cassock Suggests 'Moral Problems'," *LifeSiteNews*, Friday September 27, 2019, https://www.lifesitenews.com/news/pope-criticizes-young-traditional-priests-clothes-cassock-means-moral-problems.

the good of their fellow Catholics regardless of whatever liturgy they attend.

For the purposes of this book, we will define a traditionalist Catholic as a person who desires to see the traditions of the Church continued, practiced, and handed down to future generations. This includes desiring the Church's rich history in her doctrine, liturgy, and disciplines to be restored after their temporary abandonment following the Second Vatican Council. Underneath this umbrella, there are a wide variety of individuals, even some who might never have considered themselves as traditionalists. During this current crisis within the Church, anyone who is in favor of tradition is on the same side. Whether he realizes it or not, he is a traditional Catholic. If, out of fear of being labeled rigid, judgmental, crazy, or disobedient to the pope, you do not feel comfortable associating with people who call themselves traditionalists, it is my hope that after reading this work, your perspective will change. For we traditionalists are loyal to Holy Mother Church, the Ark of Salvation.

Ave Maria Purissima.

—Kenneth Alexander

INTRODUCTION

On April 15, 2019, Notre Dame Cathedral was set ablaze. There were a variety of reactions to such a shocking and tragic moment in history. Some questioned the official narrative that the fire was an accident and instead claimed that it was an act of terrorism. Others viewed the fire from a purely secular perspective, remarking how France was losing one of its national landmarks. There was one group of people, however, that stood out from the others. This group stood and watched as Notre Dame burned, praying and singing hymns in honor of the church, the Virgin Mary, and God. This book is addressed to this demographic.

After the blaze finally subsided, firefighters explored the interior of the cathedral and filed a damage report. Despite flames that could be felt from the opposite side of the river Seine, the interior of the church was left largely unscathed. The roof caved in on the modern table altar, but the traditional altar was still standing and left largely untouched.[1] As a result, the first Mass held at Notre Dame after the fire had to be celebrated *ad orientem* (priest and people facing "to the east"), which is how the

---

[1] Greg Maresca, "Purification of Notre Dame by Fire," *The Remnant*, April 20, 2019, https://remnantnewspaper.com/web /index.php/fetzen-fliegen/item/4439-sifting-through-the -ashes-reflection-on-notre-dame-as-warning-sign.

traditional Mass has always been celebrated, as opposed to *versus populum* (priest facing "toward the people").

One cannot help but connect the enduring traditional altar of the burned Notre Dame Cathedral to the Church's current state. Sadly, many laity and clergy, especially at the Vatican, have been accused of the worst sins imaginable. Whether it stems from sexual abuse, financial inconsistencies, heterodox teachings, murder, blasphemy, or even outright apostasy, there is not one sin left untried in the modern Church. Yes, the Catholic Church, by all appearances, is analogously burning down, just as Notre Dame Cathedral appeared to be burning completely to the ground. However, just as Notre Dame did not become a pile of ashes but rather only suffered losses to some of her newer additions (the spire, the modern altar), the Church survived due to its solid support: Sacred Tradition. Like Notre Dame's medieval stone buttresses that kept the structure from collapsing in on itself by resisting the flames, so also with Sacred Tradition—her timeless beliefs will preserve the Church in the face of modernity's fiery attacks.

The analogy of flames attacking and burning the Church is not my own but was uttered by the pontiff largely considered the first modern pope: Paul VI. When discussing the aftermath of Vatican II, the pontiff remarked, "Through some mysterious crack—no it's not mysterious; through some crack, the smoke of Satan has entered the Church of God."[2] That smoke turned into a flame, and that flame has become a raging fire.

---

[2]   Paul VI, General Audience on the Feast of the Martyrdom of Peter and Paul, June 29, 1972.

What is the fire? Identifying the crisis in the visible Church is not the struggle; rather, the struggle is trying to find which portions of the Church *are not* engulfed by the flames of scandal. Unfortunately, the wildfire has spread far and wide. The most infamous scandal involves the former cardinal Theodore McCarrick. Perhaps you might be offended that I referred to McCarrick as a cardinal, albeit formerly, since he has now been disgraced and defrocked. However, it is important to recognize that he once held one of the highest ranking positions in the American Church. Mr. McCarrick has been credibly accused of grooming, seducing, and abusing young seminarians while he was in a position of power over them.[3] He also has been accused of molesting minors while serving in New York. In his interviews with Michael Voris and Dr. Taylor Marshall, Mr. James Grein (the most well-known victim of McCarrick) discussed how the former cardinal abused him during the sacrament of confession.

McCarrick's behavior is absolutely disgusting, vile, and a tragedy. But why is this so important? This is just one area of the Church that is fallen, and besides, there are similar rates of sexual abuse in other secular and religious institutions in comparison to the Catholic Church![4] It is

---

[3]   Christine Niles, "High-Ranking US Cardinal Accused of Sex Abuse," *Church Militant*, June 20th, 2018.

[4]   William O'Donohue, Olga Cirlugea, and Lorraine Benuto, "Some Key Misunderstandings Regarding the Child Sexual Abuse Scandal and the Catholic Church," *Catholic League*, April 27, 2012, https://www.catholicleague.org/some-key -misunderstandings-regarding-the-child-sexual-abuse-scandal -and-the-catholic-church/.

sad and horrible but nothing to lose sleep over, or so the logic goes. I have heard Catholics use this line of reasoning to brush away instances of abuse in the Church. I used this very same argument after I came back to the Faith and was confronted about the abuse crisis of the early 2000s. This line of argumentation does not work any longer; Catholics must stop making excuses and look at the state of the Church for what it is. We must not become complacent.

If one were to argue that Mr. McCarrick is an extreme exception to the general norm and that we can ignore that scenario as an unusual blip in an overall healthy Church, he would be mistaken. The Pennsylvania grand jury report was a bombshell investigation into sexual abuse in six Catholic dioceses within the state. The investigation found that 301 priests sexually abused more than 1,000 children, with 80 percent of the victims being post-pubescent boys.[5] The abuse is terrifying in and of itself, but the details of the abuse are even more disturbing, turning into an entirely separate category of sin known as diabolical.

Diabolical sins are beyond vile and perverted. They scandalize souls and blaspheme God's created natural order, and they cry out for his vengeance. For instance, some perverted priests of the modern Church would use whips and sadism on their victims, blaspheme by placing their victims on crosses while taking pictures of them,

---

[5]   Stephen Wynne, "Pennsylvania Grand Jury Report: One Year Later," *Church Militant*, August 14, 2019, https://www.church militant.com/news/article/pennsylvania-grand-jury-report-one -year-later.

and mark their victims with golden crosses so other priests could spot them as they traveled throughout the dioceses.

Despite these damning reports, many leading Catholic intellectuals, clergy, and hierarchy think that the Church is fine. Moreover, many lay people lack righteous anger, resulting in relatively little accountability from their shepherds or no attempts at identifying the root causes of these atrocities. Many Catholics have read about the sexual abuse scandals but then seem to keep quiet, resembling Pope Francis's statement that he would "not speak one word" when asked about his knowledge of these events. Surprisingly, numerous Catholics have acknowledged the abuse crisis but fail to investigate it further since they are afraid of what they might find.

Additionally, some Catholics become angry or judgmental toward those members who report on these issues and demand change. They argue that investigative Catholics do not use the right tone when they condemn diabolical satanic pederasts. Sadly, the faithful Catholics who speak out against clerical sexual abuse seem to be the minority while those who dismiss these reports, ignoring the blatant truth, appear to be the majority. When the minority is criticized for their tone—that is, for speaking the truth—their naysayers ought to recall Christ's words concerning those who abuse children: yes, these people should have a millstone tied around their neck and thrown into the bottom of the sea (see Mt 18:6).

Before we discuss how the laity have been affected by this corruption, let us highlight two more instances of sexual scandal. In the last paragraph, I used the word *satanic* to describe the abusers. This was not hyperbolic language. These men were either satanic in their actions or outright Satanists who wanted to destroy the Church. As our Lord stated, whoever is not for him is against him, and the main adversary of Christ is Satan. Two further examples of literal Satanism that have occurred in the Church illustrate my point. One example occurred by an Idaho priest named W. Thomas Faucher who supposedly urinated in the communion wine and admitted to being attracted to Satanism.[6] On top of these diabolical acts of blasphemy and utter vulgarism, he was also arrested and sentenced for twenty-five years on charges of child pornography.

The second example is from another "Prince of the Church," former cardinal Joseph Bernardin of the Archdiocese of Chicago. The cardinal had a long track record of supporting liberal ideas: he received the highest medal a civilian can receive by President Bill Clinton, he supported homosexual movements such as "Call to Action," and he was written about glowingly by the homosexual newspaper *The Washington Blade*.[7] By complete coincidence, the former cardinal has also been credibly accused of being a satanic rapist. Go figure. A document

---

[6]   Katy Moeller and Ruth Brown, "Boise Priest Who Lived In 'World of Satanism And Pornography' Sentenced To 25 Years in Prison," *Idaho Statesman*, December 20, 2018, https://www.idahostatesman.com/news/local/crime/article223358745.html.

[7]   "Bernardin: Homosexual Predator Satanist," *Church Militant*, June 26, 2019, https://www.churchmilitant.com/news/article/bernardin-homosexual-predator-satanist.

uncovered from the vaults of Chicago's archdiocese by *Church Militant* stated that on June 18, 1993, a young woman accused then Father Bernardin and Bishop Russel of raping her as part of a satanic ritual.[8] This occurred while Bernardin was in Charleston, South Carolina. Despite this lady's testimony (one of many against Bernardin), various bishops, and even Pope John Paul II, took no action against him as he moved up the ranks, becoming a cardinal.

Do we smell the smoke? Do we see the flames now? It only gets worse when you turn to matters of the Faith, especially when you look at the laity's understanding of Church teaching. A recent Pew Research Center survey found that half of American Catholics believe that the Eucharist is merely a symbol, and only a third of Catholics believe in the Real Presence of Christ in the Eucharist.[9] You could be optimistic and say "Hey, look! The glass is half full!" But this would be a mistake since the Eucharist has been defined as the source and summit of the Catholic Faith.[10] It is hard to imagine what other vital issues they are at odds with if only half of the United States Catholics believe in the *source and summit of the Faith.*

Unfortunately, you do not have to imagine what these other issues might be. A plethora of Pew Research

---

[8]   Ibid.

[9]   Marshall Connolly, "What? Only One-Third of US Catholics Say They Believe in the True Presence," *Catholic Online*, August 12, 2019, https://www.catholic.org/news/hf/faith/story.php?id=82389.

[10] *Catechism of the Catholic Church*, no. 1324.

Center surveys reveal the extent of heterodox teachings in the modern American Church: 62 percent of Catholics believe Communion should be given to people who have been divorced and remarried without an annulment.[11] Only a third of Catholics believe homosexual behavior is sinful.[12] Over half of Catholics believe abortion should be legal in nearly all circumstances, and over 75 percent of Catholics believe that contraception should be permitted.[13]

Everything which I have just stated is only about one country in the Catholic world. The book *Index of Leading Catholic Indicators: The Church Since Vatican II* found sharp declines in Mass attendance, baptisms, religious ordinations, and even Catholic High Schools, and the state of the Faith in Europe is at least as grim.[14] If you

---

[11]   Michael Lipka, "Most U.S. Catholics Hope for Change in Church Rule on Divorce, Communion," *Pew Research Center*, October 26, 2015, https://www.pewresearch.org/fact-tank/20 15/10/26/most-u-s-catholics-hope-for-change-in-church-rule -on-divorce-communion/.

[12]   Michael Lipka, "U.S. Catholics More Hopeful Than Expectant of Changes to Church Teachings," *Pew Research Center*, March 12, 2014, https://www.pewresearch.org/fact-tank/2014/03/12 /u-s-catholics-more-hopeful-than-expectant-of-changes-to -church-teachings/.

[13]   Michael Lipka, "Vatican Synod on Family Highlights Discord Between Church Teachings and U.S. Catholics' Views," *Pew Research Center*, October 3, 2014, https://www.pewresearch.org /fact-tank/2014/10/03/vatican-synod-on-family-highlights -discord-between-church-teachings-and-u-s-catholics-views -2/.

[14]   Kenneth C. Jones, *Index of Leading Catholic Indicators: The Church Since Vatican II* (St. Louis: Oriens Publishing, 2003).

do look to the global Church to try and find hope, you will be met with even more scandals, such as the Vatican favoring the Communist state-sponsored Church over the devotional and persecuted underground churches in China, and the confusing ecological ritual which took place during the Amazon Synod.

It appears there is very little hope for the Church. Yes, the Church's current state is analogous to the first reports of Notre Dame being set ablaze. At the time, many feared it would be completely burned to the ground and erased from history. After reading the first pages of this book, it is hard not to assume the same thing is happening to the Church as a whole. Satanists have entered the highest Church positions, disturbing and vile sexual abuse has occurred at their hands, Catholic morality is being rejected, and even the pope has made statements that have caused confusion and doubt. All hope seems lost, and the Church looks like she is about to be burned to ashes.

But looks can be deceiving. Christ himself stated that all these tribulations would occur before his second coming. He said, "But yet the Son of Man, when he cometh, shall he find, think you, faith on earth?" (Lk 18:8). He also promised that the gates of hell shall not prevail against his Church (see Mt 16:18). As Catholics, we have an obligation to cling to both Scripture and tradition, to offer up sacrifices as well as penances in reparation for the failures within Church leadership, to resist false teaching and to seek what is objectively true, beautiful, and good.

But what path should Catholics take? How does one remain securely on the bark of Peter when she appears to be sinking from implosion? How can one possibly keep the Church afloat and protect her from foes? While I do not claim to have all the answers, I do know that continuing down the path we are on is self-destructive. There are some voices in the Church suggesting we should shun tradition and instead change the core of the Church. One of the great influencers of this attitude in the Church was Cardinal Martini, who famously expressed before his death, "The Church is two hundred years behind the times. Why is she not shaken up? Are we afraid? Fear, instead of courage?"[15] Something similar to this mindset has also been voiced more recently by Pope Francis in a Christmas address to the Roman Curia:

> Linked to this difficult historical process there is always the temptation to fall back on the past (also by employing new formulations), because it is more reassuring, familiar, and, to be sure, less conflictual. This too is part of the process and risk of setting in motion significant changes. Here, there is a need to be wary of the temptation to rigidity. A rigidity born of the fear of change, which ends up erecting fences and obstacles on the terrain of the common good, turning it into a minefield of incomprehension and hatred. Let us always remember that behind every form of rigidity lies some kind of imbalance. Rigidity and imbalance feed one another in a vicious circle. And today this temptation to rigidity has become very real.[16]

---

15   Peter Kwasniewski, "Pope Francis's Hermeneutic of Anti-Continuity," *The Remnant*, December 22, 2019, https://remnantnews paper.com/web/index.php/articles/item/4708-pope-francis -s-hermeneutic-of-anti-continuity.

16   Ibid.

If this is the diagnosis, then it seems as if we have misunderstood the real crisis facing the Church. If we think the solution to the current crisis is to continue abandoning tradition, then we are on the wrong path. Tradition is the answer to the problems that are plaguing the Church. Does this mean we need to remove everything that is considered new in the Church? Not at all; in fact, Notre Dame's Golden Cross from the 1970s survived the fire. Hence, anything in the modern Church that does not contradict but helps enhance Sacred Tradition should be celebrated and encouraged. But we should also be aware that there have been numerous additions to the Church which have been detrimental to the faithful and must be replaced with tradition.

For instance, the modern Church is facing a crisis in vocations, a lack of male attendance of all ages at Mass, a lack of youth attendance, and there is a crisis in understanding the basics of Catholic doctrine. In churches that use traditional liturgies and devotions, these issues disappear. A recent study found that while Novus Ordo (that is, the 1969 Mass of Pope Paul VI) parishes have been shrinking, traditional parishes have been growing.[17] Another study found that the average traditional parish has larger family sizes, younger attendees, and higher male attendance.[18] While the modern Church painfully

---

[17] Jeffrey Cimmino, "Traditional Catholic Parishes Grow Even as US Catholicism Declines," *Washington Examiner*, November 2, 2019, https://www.washingtonexaminer.com/news/traditional-catholic-parishes-grow-even-as-us-catholicism-declines.

[18] Joseph Shaw, "The Extraordinary Form and the Evangelization of Men," *Foederatio Internationalis Una Voce*, position paper

attempts to reach the youth with guitar Masses and rock songs, young Catholics find themselves enthralled with the Traditional Latin Mass. The most recent example of young Catholics embracing tradition was seen at the National Catholic Youth Conference of 2019 when the Solemn High Mass at St. John's, the church located right across from the conference center, was packed.[19]

Not only is tradition able to assist the Church by attracting the laity of every age and sex, but it is also able to help solve the vocation crisis. Traditional orders have seen an increase in the number of priestly ordinations, and female religious vocations have also been aided by traditional devotions. For example, an order of nuns in the United States turned from the modern innovations of Vatican II back to their pre-conciliar devotions and the results were astounding: "The Discalced Carmelites have turned from the modern Church's reforms of the 1960s and embraced ancient traditions—particularly the traditional Latin Mass. Now their order is booming, with multiple at-capacity monasteries dotting the eastern U.S."[20] Just as with the Notre Dame Cathedral, the Church's newer additions are being burned away, but the

---

no.26, September 3, 2012.

[19]   Gregory Dipippo, "Tradition is for the Young: EF Mass at the National Catholic Youth Conference," *New Liturgical Movement*, November 29, 2019, https://www.new liturgicalmovement.org/2019/11/tradition-is-for-young-ef -mass-at.html#.YWRBqS9h1mA.

[20]   Drew Belsky, "Latin Mass, Church Traditions Bring Boom in Vocations for US Order of Nuns," *LifeSiteNews*, Aug 13, 2019, https://www.lifesitenews.com/news/latin-mass-church-trad itions-bring-boom-in-vocations-for-us-order-of-nuns.

traditional practices serve as the buttresses to protect the Church from collapsing in on itself.

In the following pages, you will see the beauty of tradition as a clear path to sanctity. You will see the hope that the Church has in her future. You will see how I went from a cafeteria Catholic to a traditional Catholic. You will see how I went from only attending Mass on Christmas and Easter to attending Mass every Sunday, and even attending daily Mass. You will see how I went from being skeptical of tradition to attending the Traditional Latin Mass almost exclusively. You will see stories like mine from young, joyful Catholics across the country, with the same unifying belief in tradition, and you will see that abandoning the Deposit of Faith in favor of modern adaptations to make the Church "relevant" will be her suicide. The future of the Church lies in her past.

—Kenneth Alexander

CHAPTER 1

THE COUNTER-REVOLUTION

In the early morning of October 21, 2019, statues were removed from the Church of Santa Maria in Traspontina and were thrown into the Tiber River. To any Catholic unaware of what I am referring to, this might sound like a terrible act of sacrilege and theft. However, these statues were not Catholic statues; instead, they depicted the topless and pregnant Peruvian fertility goddess known as Pachamama. Shortly after the incident, a video was released from an anonymous source of two young men destroying these idols in front of the Castle of Saint Michael the Archangel. Various high-ranking members of the Church came out and supported this action, including Bishop Athanasius Schneider, Cardinal Raymond Leo Burke, and Cardinal Walter Brandmüller. They all argued that these idols never should have been allowed in a Catholic Church. The following interview is with one of the brave men behind this action, Alexander Tschugguel. Since this incident, Alexander has founded the Saint Boniface Institute. The institute is named for Saint Boniface who, according to tradition, cut down an oak tree being worshiped by pagans and used the wood to build a church.

* * *

Could you please describe your family and your upbringing?
I was born in 1993, and I am twenty-six years old. I was raised in Vienna, Austria. My father is a doctor of medicine and my mother is a psychologist. In total, I have three older sisters, but one died shortly after she was born. My Protestant father emergency baptized her before her death, so we can be sure that she is in heaven, which is a relief.

How did you come to the Catholic faith?
I came into the Catholic faith at fifteen years old on the fifteenth of June 2009. From the age of fourteen, I had plenty of questions about Protestantism that I was not receiving very good answers to. I was not very strong in my Protestant faith. My great grandfather converted to Protestantism, and he was the first one in my family. Protestantism was (thankfully) a short-lived experience for my family.

Catholicism came into my life through many false and strange teachings by my religion teacher. This teacher took my class to the local Catholic Church and showed us a sign which discussed an apparent indulgence available for the parishioners. The indulgence was being granted to the faithful for All-Saints day, but my teacher taught us, "It looks like the same thing has occurred since Luther's time: they still expect you to pay for indulgences!" I looked at the sign, however, and I saw nothing about having to make any payments. This angered me, so I decided to call a priest and schedule a conversation with him.

Luckily for me, the priest was very logical and well versed in the Faith! I asked him questions about the papacy, indulgences, the Holy Mass, and for every one of my questions, he had an answer for me which made sense! I told my parents about this conversation and how I was planning on becoming Catholic. They were very disappointed to hear this, but they also told me they loved me and wanted to support me in this decision if it was what I thought was best. It was after this conversation that I entered the Church. It was only after converting to the Faith that I realized the magnitude of my decision. The Faith is immense and complex, and I was overwhelmed.

Once you became Catholic, did you have a transition from the Novus Ordo to the Traditional Latin Mass or have you always been traditional in your faith?

I had a transition. My conversion to the Church was very conservative but Novus Ordo. For instance, I have never received Communion in the hand, and I was always instructed to kneel to receive Communion. To further demonstrate how conservative these priests were, the first Mass I attended was a traditional Mass. I agreed to have my first Mass be a traditional Mass because I was raised in a very conservative household, so I figured traditional would be best. I must admit, however, I thought it was a little bit boring. (Laughs) No one explained it to me!

After this Mass, I discussed with the priest how the traditional liturgy worked, but I was still confused. It took me a few years to fully accept the traditional aspects of the Faith. I was very involved in the church community and was growing in my Faith. I began reading many different sources about the Catholic worldview. I eventually came across a book which allowed me to transition from the Novus Ordo to the traditional Mass. The book is called *Revolution and Counter Revolution* by Professor Plinio Correa de Oliveira. Oliveira was a Brazilian academic and politician who discussed the nature of liberal revolutions in society. It was by reading this book that I began to connect Church history with the writings of Oliveira.

Oliveira discussed how liberal revolutions wanted to remove hierarchical order from society, in fact, to remove all order from society. Order comes from God, and so the liberals hate it. I cannot recommend this book enough; the English version is very good.

To be more specific, reckless alteration of the liturgy and the abandonment of the Church's traditions are completely consistent with revolutionary strategies. If the Novus Ordo was instituted by revolutionaries, then it was my duty as a Catholic to support the Catholic counter-revolution. And it was very important for me to realize that the counter-revolution is not our revolution. The counter-revolution is not about what I want or what you want but ultimately about what God desires. The counter-revolution is devoted to what existed before the revolution, and this applies both politically and liturgically.

It was due to Oliveira that I began attending the traditional Mass again and appreciating its beauty! I consider myself a traditionalist now, but it took some time for me to transition from my Novus Ordo parish. This occurred in the year 2014. I eventually learned how to serve the traditional Mass, and ever since then, I have absolutely fallen in love with traditionalism and the way things have always been in the Church.

What are some of your favorite traditional devotions? What does your prayer life look like?
What I truly love about the traditional life is the Low Mass. (For readers who are unaware, the Low Mass is the form of the Latin Mass which is said without a choir or chant and is mostly said in a hushed tone). I love how this Mass is practically silent during the week. Silence is such a grace. Throughout the week, you are plagued with noise and distraction; when you go to Mass, you should be given silence, mystery, and sacrifice. There is such beauty in this Mass, and it was entirely removed by the Novus Ordo.

I was also truly blown away by comparing the traditional prayers of the liturgy with the Novus Ordo. I began attending pre-1955 liturgies during Holy Week, and every single prayer and motion had intelligibility behind them. Attending a Novus Ordo Mass and a pre-1955 liturgy is a completely different experience.[1]

---

[1]   For readers who are unaware, pre-1955 Holy Weeks were unaltered by the man who would go on to gut the Traditional Mass and create the Novus Ordo, Annibale Bugnini.

Then I began attending Mass with a 1962 missal, and even when I compared the 1962 liturgy with the one we had before 1955, I could find many differences. It is my opinion that the Church ought to return to the unaltered liturgy of pre-1955. What I saw at this liturgy changed my understanding of the Catholic faith. So many traditions, prayers, and devotions of our Faith come from the liturgy, and they all make sense and come together once you attend a traditional Mass.

Attending the traditional Mass has allowed me to increase my prayer life at home. I pray Morning Prayer when I get the chance, but every night, I pray Evening Prayer with my wife. The traditional liturgy matches beautifully with the Liturgy of the Hours. Included in the Evening Prayers is a Sacred Heart devotion, which in German nineteenth-century language uses words which rhyme with one another. It is truly a beautiful habit that we have developed. Another devotion which we have is the Saint Michael's Prayer.[2] My wife is trying to learn it by heart in Latin, which I did a few years ago.

Another traditional devotion which we have gained from the traditional Mass is the Rosary. When I first entered the Faith, I thought the Rosary was a very feminine devotion, but I was mistaken. The traditional understanding of the Rosary is that it is a weapon given to us by God through our Lady to help us destroy the serpent. Now, everywhere I go, I have a Rosary in my

---

[2]   Again, for any readers who do not know, Pope Leo XIII commissioned the Saint Michael prayer to be read after every Low Mass due to a vision he had of demons descending on Rome. This prayer was removed by the Novus Ordo.

pocket, which is something new in my life. I recommend this practice—always carry one with you wherever you go. Also be sure to pray it every day!

One devotion which I have enjoyed is finding local patron saints and asking for their intercession. For instance, I have sought the aid of Blessed Karl of Austria, Saint Leopold, and the long tradition of Austrian saints, emperors, and leaders. There are a host of wonderful Catholic military figures to pray to known as the Rosary generals. These military heroes always fought their battles with a rosary in their hands. One amazing example was a man named Andreas Hofer (1767–1810), who fought Napoleon's troops and removed them from Austria. He was betrayed by the Bavarians, but he overcame their betrayal and fought valiantly. Another was known as Prince Eugen of Savoy (1663–1736). He was Italian, French, and a little bit German. He was considered too small to be helpful to the king of France, but the Holy Roman emperor found use for him in repelling the Turks from their siege of Vienna. Nowadays, modern historians have bought into propaganda that he was a homosexual, which I find extremely disappointing and a lie. A lot of military men in Europe would be later labelled as homosexuals because they practiced celibacy during their military duties.

Celibacy was a military discipline; leaders were expected to stay celibate during military service so that they could devote themselves entirely to the cause if they were in the active fight. This same reality occurs in the Church because the priests are in spiritual warfare against the devil and his demons. Priests must be totally devoted to the cause, far more than any soldier who fights in physical wars. Celibacy is an essential spiritual discipline of the Church, which must be safeguarded.

The traditional Faith teaches us that we must all connect our vocation with fighting the devil and his wicked ways; we must fight for the good, *whatever it is that we do*. God puts you in this life for a reason. There is a reason you exist here and now. And I think the saints and historical figures I described above are perfect examples of that mindset.

Why do you think traditional Catholicism is growing, especially among young people?
Yes, this is a very easy question! Nothing is fixed in the modern world—this strange world—not even your sexual and biological identity! People naturally know this is wrong. Once they recognize how unnatural the leftist revolutionary lies about biology, sexuality, and order are, they are well on their way to discovering the Faith. They are now looking to reality, which is where you will find the God of reality. The natural order is hierarchical, intelligently ordered, and it is fixed. The Traditional Latin Mass matches reality, truth, order, and it is *fixed*.[3]

The younger generation needs to understand and discover the difference between freedom and license. The freedom we have as human beings is huge; we can freely choose our actions and whether we want to follow God or not. This freedom does not excuse our actions;

---

[3]   Here, Alexander does not mean fixed as in entirely permanent. The traditional liturgy experiences organic growth.

however, we do not have the right to freely ignore the truth—that would be license. When we act according to license, we suffer immensely. It is impossible to willingly act against the truth and not suffer greatly. There are two choices: order and disorder.

This same choice happens in the liturgy. Now, Novus Ordo Masses aren't necessarily chaotic. I have met many people who attend reverent Novus Ordo Masses. But the ones which are reverent are the ones which *try* to match the traditional Mass as much as possible. They are not reverent because of the Novus Ordo; they are reverent because they include tradition in their liturgies. But as soon as there is a part in the Mass where priests can be revolutionary, then they will tend towards the revolution. This is because they have the freedom to do so. I will give an example: the priest at my conversion parish was very conservative. But during the Christmas Mass, he brought in a table altar to face *versus populum* rather than *ad orientem* for the Catholics who only attend Mass once a year. He would do this because *he could*, he had the option. It was very strange, but it allowed me to come to the conclusion that you can never receive the full tradition from attending the Novus Ordo Mass; it is inherently lacking.

You can celebrate the Novus Ordo reverently, but this just proves the point that reverent Novus Ordo Masses are just Masses that *approach* the traditional Mass and reflect its truth, beauty, and goodness. But they can never match the traditional Mass and its prayers. I will give you an analogy: Imagine what it is like when you have guests coming to your house for dinner. You clean your house thoroughly: You scrub your floors, you clean nooks you have not cleaned since the last time you had guests, and you do everything you possibly can to make your house presentable. And when your guests are there, you do everything in your power to ensure that the guests have a good time and enjoy their stay.

Now, imagine God is coming to your house. You would try to do everything the absolute best way possible when he came to visit. The effort and dedication you took to cleaning your home would be amplified tenfold. You would serve him and anticipate anything he might need or require for him to enjoy his stay. You would never accept a 90 percent devotion to him as your guest, you would never deliberately leave out gestures or reverence to him as your guest. If you would not accept a 90 percent devotion, would you accept a 30 percent devotion? Of course not! So why would we do this when we are worshiping God and his sacrifice on the altar? Archbishop Bugnini removed most of the prayers from the traditional Roman Missal.[4] The Mass is about serving God, not yourself, yet we are choosing to deliberately give him less than he deserves for the sake of our own comfort. This does not make any sense.

The youth want to place religion before and above emotionalism. Secularism presents our youth with the

---

[4]   According to Dr. Kwasniewski it was 83 percent of the prayers for the Traditional Mass which were removed during the implementation of the Novus Ordo. Peter Kwasniewski, "A Half-Century of Novelty: Revisiting Paul VI's Apologia for the New Mass," *Rorate Caeli*, April 4, 2019, https://rorate-caeli.blog spot.com/2019/04/a-half-century-of-novelty-revisiting.html.

option of emotionalism. If the younger generations wanted this, then they would merely be secular. Yet, despite this, the Novus Ordo tends to flip this order on its head. It gives into and surrenders to the Zeitgeist, to the spirit of the age. Saint Paul warned us about this in his letter to the Romans, I believe it was in chapter 12 that he stated, "And be not conformed to this world: but be reformed in the newness of your mind, that you may prove what is the good and the acceptable and the perfect will of God."[5] We have largely abandoned the advice of Saint Paul and surrendered the Church to the spirit of the age, and I believe the Novus Ordo reflects this abandonment.

Tell us about the Saint Boniface Institute. What was your inspiration for making this institute and what are your goals for this project?
I created the Saint Boniface Institute to release the videos of the removal of the Pachamamas. My friend and I knew that we had support for what we did with the Pachamama statues, but we did not want to take credit for this action. We wanted the act to speak for itself, without people behind the actions. Since then, I have decided to step out and reveal myself as having done this. On May 13, 2020, Saint Boniface Institute will be hosting a conference in Vienna. This conference will reveal the next steps of the Saint Boniface Institute after saying a Rosary, a Eucharistic procession, and of course the traditional Mass. While I will not go into too much

---

5   Romans 12:2.

detail now, I will let you know that our goals are aimed at academic research, uniting Catholics, and restoring Christendom.

If you could have a conversation with a Catholic who disagreed with your actions during the Amazon Synod, what would you say to them? Can't we just baptize the Pachamama statues into the Catholic Faith?
It's okay for people to disagree with what I did. It is especially okay if they themselves would not have spiritually felt called to do what I did. The reason they are Catholic is through their prayer life. If people reject what I did, then that's okay. Please follow Christ and do not follow me. Every fight has divisions and groups; the military is divided into different battalions. In the Church, it is the same way: some have talents of being in the background, saying prayers silently and behind closed doors, while others have talents to do the kind of actions that I did. The people who disagree with what I did typically do not care for the politics of the Church and just want to cultivate their relationship with the Lord.

If everyone supported me, it would be much more shocking. People should act according to the talents God gave them, and he does not expect everyone to join the public fight. I received the idea for this action from prayer, and I consulted priests and my wife before I did this. It was not done purely out of emotion or impulse. If anyone is skeptical of what I did on that day, judge my actions based on the fruits they have borne. Bishops, priests, and laity from around the world have written me letters and reached out to me telling me how my actions aided their faith and hope. If my actions have led others to Christ, then I ask those who are skeptical of my actions to use this as the metric for their skepticism.

The second half of this question is very important. We cannot baptize purely pagan ideas into Catholicism. There is only *one truth*. Everything someone says is either the truth or falsehood. It is our duty to give God what is good and in conformity to the truth. As Catholics, there are certain statements and actions which we must accept as true. For instance: there is nothing that is created which is also God. Only the Creator is God. Everything which was created must not receive worship but must bow in submission to the one true God. The idea of Pachamama goes against this understanding of our Faith, the idea of bowing down to a representation of Mother Earth goes entirely against only offering worship to God.

We do not enculturate errors, and the following is a perfect example. You would not enculturate an immigrant's broken English into the English language; you would teach him the proper way to speak English. If he said to you, "Job I need for money, me hire you for job," you would correct his sentence and teach him proper English. This is merciful and charitable. We would not conform the English language to his error. There would be no way to enculturate his mistakes into the language. If we do this for human language, we must do it for moral and divine language. Catholics must adhere to all the commandments, especially not bearing false witness and having strange gods before God.

As I said before, the idea of Pachamama is that creation is a deity and it ought to be worshiped. You cannot cultivate ideas which are not true to the Catholic Church; you cannot baptize falsehood. And the belief in Pachamama is false. It would be cruel and uncharitable to encourage others to continue this false belief. Our job as Catholics is not to hug people who cling to false religions and tell them everything is alright. This would be wrong; we have an obligation to convert these people to what is the truth.

Thank you, Alexander, for a wonderful interview. Let us close in prayer.
In Latin!

Yes, let's pray the Our Father.
In nomine Patris et Filii et Spiritús Sancti. Pater Noster qui es in caelis, sanctificetur nomen tuum. Adveniat regnum tuum. Fiat voluntas tua, sicut in caelo et in terra. Panem nostrum quotidianum da nobis hodie, et dimitte nobis debita nostra, sicut et nos dimittimus debitoribus nostris. Et ne nos inducas in tentationem sed libera nos a malo. Amen.

CHAPTER 2

THE LITURGY OF THE AGES

My name is David Dashiell, and I am a twenty-five-year-old Catholic. I was raised near Baltimore, Maryland, and I was raised Catholic. My temperament is naturally oriented toward rules, routine, ideals, and worship, and I took to the Faith quickly. Because my mother was my only committed Catholic parent, the Faith did not have much of an influence on my life. My education in Catholicism was limited to Sunday Mass, weekly religion classes, and youth group. Most of what I heard had to do with fundamental prayers, Scripture passages, and conversational prayer with Jesus—not bad, but not substantial. As I continued to pursue God and grow in my faith, I decided to study theology and catechetics at Franciscan University of Steubenville, Ohio. At the time, I wanted to be a youth minister. That and the priesthood were practically all I knew of my options for work in the Catholic world, but I was passionate enough about the Faith to orient my life toward spreading it, even if I didn't understand it well.

At the time, I didn't realize how little I knew. After a visit to the university, I began to read a book called *Aquinas' Shorter Summa*, a simplified version of the *Summa Theologiae* that Saint Thomas began to write but never completed. It took me months to read, with each paragraph lasting about a half an hour. I was known as a good student and I thought deeply about the world, but diving into the Angelic Doctor's work without knowing a thing about Scholasticism meant that I was in over my head. I was interested, though, and continued to study philosophical and theological works on my own time throughout college. As I progressed at Franciscan, I realized that there was a whole Catholic world that I had never been exposed to. My childhood experience was not unlike that of many others my age: I had received a shallow Catholicism, a hand-me-down from the Baby Boomers and the generations surrounding them. It was as if nothing happened in the Catholic Church before 1962, liturgically or theologically. Not that anyone looked down on the pre-Vatican II Church explicitly; it was simply not mentioned. Prior to attending Franciscan University, I couldn't have told you about any popes or theologians before Saint John Paul II, except for Saint Peter and the other apostles.

In the early years of my studies, I dabbled in charismatic prayer. It felt foreign to me as an introverted and academically oriented Catholic, but I thought that I should give it a try. I attended seminars on "Baptism in the Holy Spirit," went to praise and worship sessions, and occasionally attended a "Festival of Praise," which included a talk, a band, and an intense adoration experience. These experiences became more comfortable to me, but I could never shake the feeling that some of the people involved in these practices appeared to be riding on emotional highs. I believed (and believe) in miracles, healings, and the rest, and I respected those who claimed to have profound prayer experiences. But as I continued, I could not ignore the vapid songs and surface-level praise. Many of those involved in charismatic prayer were too interested in chasing intense experiences and acquiring spiritual gifts that were supposed to be given freely by God. There were honest, pious, charismatic Catholics, but overall, I did not see much depth.

It was around this time that I got involved in the university's liturgy committee tasked with recruiting, training, and scheduling liturgical ministers for the university. I began as co-head of ushers and served on the committee for three years, coordinating lectors and extraordinary ministers of Holy Communion, working summer youth and adult conferences, and acting as the chapel assistant. There, I met a solid group of faithful, attractive, and intelligent Catholics who shared some of my views about prayer, worship, and liturgy. These individuals and my professors taught me a great deal about the Church. I continued to have issues with liturgical music and priests who would hijack the Mass to shift the focus to themselves, but I happily attended the Novus Ordo and assisted regularly as an extraordinary minister, lector, and usher. By the time I graduated from Franciscan University, I set my sights on a job in academia or the liturgy. I was engaged, had a Master of Arts degree in theology and Christian ministry, and had developed a specialized knowledge of and esteem for Pope Saint John Paul II's *Theology of the Body*.

My then fiancée and I moved to Nashville, Tennessee, where she was from, and I proceeded to look for work in my field. Although the closest I came was substitute teaching at various Catholic schools, we found a solid community of Catholics at a parish in Germantown. We hopped around for a while but were hard pressed to find a parish with both a vibrant community life and a reverent liturgy. We were not sure exactly what we were looking for, of course. My wife had been going to a parish run by the Priestly Fraternity of Saint Peter in Phoenix, Arizona, looking for something solid, consistent, and reverent, but she had been much more involved in the charismatic praise and worship life than I had been. I had been to the Latin Mass about ten times before moving to Nashville and was very interested, but by and large I was attending the Novus Ordo. The parish we settled on offered an *ad orientem* Novus Ordo every day but Saturday. Saturday morning was Low Mass, and Sunday morning was High Mass and then a Novus Ordo. We began to meet good, holy Catholics who identified as "trad." Some of them were overbearing or socially awkward, but for the most part, the parishioners were balanced, winsome, and fun. We took offense when many of them took potshots at the Novus Ordo, but we began to fall in love with the Latin Mass at the same time.

The Latin Mass was an otherworldly experience, celebrated with pomp and circumstance and pronounced in a different language. The music was reverent and theologically sound, and the homilies were solid. The Novus Ordo was not bad, since it was the same priest who celebrated both forms, but it did not feel quite as numinous. Life continued as usual, and a year later, I was married, about to go on a belated honeymoon, and preparing to move to Pittsburgh, Pennsylvania, to begin a job as the associate director of liturgy for a group of four Catholic churches. It was difficult to leave our friends and parish in Nashville, but we were excited that I had finally found a job in my field. We moved in late May 2019. It was bittersweet.

As I started my new job, I began to see just how bad the situation was in the Diocese of Pittsburgh, where many of the stories from the grand jury report on sexual abuse had their origin. The people were hurt, the priests were tired, and the parishes were struggling. All but two churches were in "groupings" and these two diocesan churches would eventually merge into one legal, canonical entity and one community. Also, there were two churches run by two different religious orders, which were autonomous from the diocese, and these parishes were thriving. One was run by the Oratorians of Saint Philip Neri, and the other by the Institute of Christ the King, Sovereign Priest. We had not experienced the institute before, but we had the occasion to attend a Mass celebrated by its founder and by its head for the United States very soon after we moved. We were impressed by their reverence, attention to detail, and uncompromisingly Catholic values.

Meanwhile, I was learning more and more about the Church's liturgical history and immersing myself in the baby-boomer-dominated Novus Ordo environment of the Diocese of Pittsburgh. My course on the liturgy at Franciscan University had not been very fruitful; I had barely heard anything negative or neutral about Vatican II or Annibale Bugnini, the architect of the liturgical reform in the 1950s and beyond. My catechetical studies had given me an inkling of the carnage that had followed the council, but I did not connect the dots. I had learned about the dreaded "Spirit of Vatican II" from my time on the liturgy committee, but I ardently believed what I was told about its origin: loose liturgical reforms were put into practice and morally lax doctrine was promulgated because Catholics misinterpreted the documents of Vatican II. If only the council's documents had been read properly, we would not be in this mess.

It was only after I continued my own personal research that I realized the truth was much more shocking: the Novus Ordo was developed hastily and founded on suspect principles. Bugnini might have had good intentions (although I am not sure), but by and large he ignored *centuries* of gradual and consistent liturgical development. He chose to base some additions, like Eucharistic Prayer II, on specific moments in the first centuries of the Church, moments that may or may not have transpired in the way described. Many of the other changes were based on pastoral principles that deferred to Protestant and atheistic culture. Physical, ministerial involvement of the people and a focus on convenience and community were some of the goals. The prevailing attitude seemed to be that the Church had the wrong idea from about AD 300 to 1953. Suddenly, starting with the reforms in 1954, Catholics were finally able to listen to the Holy Spirit. I recognized this attitude in some of my former classmates, the Novus Ordo by its nature, and many in the hierarchy.

Having grown to love the consistent teaching of the Church, it pained me significantly to see that since the

1950s, it had been frowned upon, not just by laity, but by many high-ranking prelates. Discovering the true power and nature of the modernism, secularism, and globalism infecting the Church made the truth, beauty, and goodness of the Latin Mass even more attractive. This attraction began during my last months of college, well before I began to realize these things about the recent history of the Church. Scandal may have urged me to research the Old Mass more quickly, but I am confident that I would have come to the same conclusions regardless of the catalyst.

Most of us have heard "trads" and "charismatics" go back and forth about Novus Ordo versus the Latin Mass, but it is helpful to see what each person loves about the Mass they attend. Regardless of how I got there, I have grown to love the Church and have found a stable home in the Latin Mass. Now that I have had the opportunity to learn from many reliable sources, I can see that the Latin Mass is not just a stable home: it is the most proper and most efficacious way to worship the Lord in the Roman rite of Catholicism.

Except for the least disposed, most people walking into a High Mass or even a Low Mass would recognize that something important is going on. Incense, bells, vestments, sacred vessels, chant, polyphony, and copious sacramentals all point to something greater than us. The priest and the people face liturgical east, signaling to visitors the significance of what is taking place on the altar. The words are spoken in Latin, a language noted for its beauty and special use by the Church. The sanctuary is raised, sectioned off, and physically set apart from the congregation, communicating that not just anyone can enter there. The congregation is not the focal point. The Sacrifice of the Mass is the focal point, and attentive visitors understand this. They may not understand it in these terms, but they understand that a sacred ritual is taking place. The fixed elements and trappings of the Mass naturally make this clear. An otherworldly atmosphere is created and put on humble yet beautiful display. Clearly, it is God who is being spoken to; the Latin Mass would go on uninterrupted if everyone outside of the sanctuary left the building. The sacrifice is offered on our behalf, but it is addressed to the Father. The people play an important part, *but they are not essential to the Mass.*[1] That is the feeling that many will experience when they encounter the Latin Mass: something important is happening up there, and everyone seems to know it. There are so many people here, but they are all focused on something different and mysterious. In fact, the priest seems to be the only one doing anything significant. Everyone else seems to be either assisting him or watching him.

This brings us to a concept popular in the Novus Ordo: active participation. Unfortunately, this phrase has come to mean participation in the liturgy through common responses, gestures, and liturgical ministries. These are

---

[1]   Contrast this with the Novus Ordo. When Annibale Bugnini was presenting the Novus Ordo to his brother bishops, someone politely remarked, "Your eminence, it seems as if you have placed so much of an emphasis on the laity at the new mass, that you have made it impossible for the mass to be said without them." To which Bugnini replied, "To be totally honest, I had not considered that. We can always add something."

not bad things, but they are not meant to be focused on exclusively. The Novus Ordo tends not to include *silence* as a method of active participation in the Mass. It is perfectly acceptable not to say anything during Mass. It is also perfectly acceptable to quietly pray a Rosary in the pew while Mass is going on. This is not disrespectful, and it does not mean that this person is not present at Mass. The point of the Mass is the sacrifice of Calvary. It re-presents this sacrifice, bringing it to the present. The merits of Christ's redemptive offering are applied to us if we participate worthily. Worthy participation does not necessarily mean being in the sanctuary or responding frequently. We must worship and adore the Lord, but one way of doing this is through attentive silence. Silence, understood in this way, is not an absence of thought or entry into a void. It is contemplation of the mystery presented to us at Mass. We allow ourselves to be assimilated into the passion, death, and resurrection of Christ. If we are aware of what is going on and are uniting our will to the priest's in offering ourselves as an oblation to the Father, we are actively participating.

This is the beautiful thing about the Latin Mass. We silently adore the Lord, attentively listening to him and desiring to be offered with him to the Father. This is what Mary did at the foot of the cross. She sat at the Lord's feet in silent adoration, contemplating his mysteries and offering herself in sober piety along with him.[2] Joining in worship with Mary and the saints is uniquely

---

[2]   See chapter 5 by Stephanie Gordon for another take on this common meditation for laity during the traditional Mass.

meaningful. We can gaze upon Christ, knowing that his sacrifice is the priority. The priest and people are facing the same direction, focusing intently on Christ's offering to the Father. As they look east, they await the return of the Lord, the Sun of Justice. Each element of the liturgy is oriented toward making this worthy sacrifice: the language, processions, chant, candles, incense, bells, vestments, genuflections, signs of the cross, invocation of the saints, and prayers speak of, prepare for, and complete this sacrifice. We do not have to speak up or cross into the sanctuary to play a more active part in the liturgy. Rather, Christ has pierced the veil and brought it to us, and he has tied his grace to the sacraments and sacramentals. If we unite our wills to his at the saving banquet which he instituted and guided, even if we are contemplating him in different ways, we can receive this grace. Whether praying a Rosary or following along in a missal, the pious and attentive participant in the Latin Mass is united to Jesus Christ.

The climax of the Mass, just like the climax of the Passion, is the moment of sacrifice, the point of death. When Christ died, silence preceded his final cry. The sky darkened and no one spoke. When the bread and wine are consecrated to become the Body and Blood of Christ, the words of the canon are spoken quietly. In silence, the priest speaks the words which bring God to earth. He comes in the flesh and offers himself, and the bells ring. The choir returns, having paused in reverence for the consecration. The Lord, present under the appearance of simple bread and wine, comes down from the altar but remains in the sanctuary. He has stooped low for us, but does not cease to be holy. Still, from the sanctuary, he is given to his people, but they must approach him worthily and humbly. We come forward and kneel, knowing that we are not worthy to encounter this mystery, let alone to receive the Lord in the flesh. We receive him on our tongues like children being fed. We stand up, strengthened and cleansed, ready to join him in heaven triumphant.

These things make me enjoy attending the Latin Mass as much as I do. In the Latin Mass, great effort is taken to create a numinous environment in keeping with what happened at Calvary. Even the architecture contributes: The altar rail and the raised marble sanctuary remind us that God is holy and not just anyone can approach him; we must be either consecrated or specially prepared. Receiving Communion kneeling and on the tongue drives the point home. The procedures and rubrics are solemn. A priest may rush through them from time to time, but this points to a failure in the priest and not in the Mass. In fact, so many gestures and prayers are fixed in the Latin Mass that the worst a priest can do short of going rogue is mumble through the Mass. There is no wiggle room for him to supplement his own prayers or replace the pious gestures with ambiguous ones.

Much of what I have said is true of both the Latin Mass and Novus Ordo, but it often seems that the Novus Ordo obscures rather than showcases these fundamental truths about the sacrifice that is happening. Those who know the history of the liturgical reforms beginning in the 1950s know that they were done hastily and with suspect principles. Again, I will leave it to more capable people to show that this is the case. The information is readily available for those who search for it. Just investigate Annibale Bugnini and his liturgical commission, along with their explicit principles for reform.

The Novus Ordo was built, in part, to encourage the active participation of the laity in the modern sense which I have described. Anyone can enter the sanctuary, and anyone can be a minister. Laypeople act as lectors, altar servers, and extraordinary ministers of Holy Communion. The Mass is reformatted to be call-and-response. There is no altar rail. The symbolism and structure suggest that the Holy of Holies is for everyone, priest or layperson, and that we are not all that different from the priest. These people contend that since Christ pierced the veil, why not pass through and get as close to him as possible? We are a royal priesthood, a nation set apart for the Lord, so why is the priest held up while the laity are not? If these things are true, shouldn't we be able to go in and out of the sanctuary, proclaiming the readings and distributing Communion? Why can't we touch the Eucharist with our hands? Receiving on the tongue is degrading.

I am not trying to mock those who appreciate the principles of the Novus Ordo. My point here is to show that the structure is suspect. Yes, Christ pierced the veil, but the Holy of Holies does not cease to be a special and sacred place. We can all enter the sanctuary, but we still must be made ready, and we have to respect the Lord and his statutes. The Holy of Holies enters us when we receive Communion. We receive the Lord on the tongue like obedient children because we recognize our unworthiness. He still comes to us; the veil is still pierced. But we still must treat him as the Lord who still dwells in unapproachable light.

Laypeople serve at the altar in the Latin Mass, but they do not proclaim the readings or distribute Communion. This is because the priest is consecrated and configured to Jesus Christ, the Head of the Church. We are a royal priesthood by our baptism, but we do not have a character that makes us a priest in the line of Melchizedek. Our hands are not consecrated. We do not follow the apostles in an unbroken line of Holy Orders. We simply do not have the power to confect the Eucharist. Even the deacon is a step removed. That is why he is the minister of the cup; touching the Host with bare hands is the function of the priest. Admitting laypeople to distribute Communion, let alone making this a regular practice, blurs the line between priest and layperson. Regardless of the intention of any given pastor, this is the message that the action sends: the priest is only unique because he says the Words of Institution. Other than that, laypeople can do most other things that he does. By contrast, the ethos of the Latin Mass sends a different message. The priest is the only one who can distribute Communion. This points to the fact that there *is* something special about him. He is conformed to Christ the Head and feeds his flock with the Eucharist just as Christ feeds his sheep with his Body and Blood.

To understand the difference between the Novus Ordo and Latin Mass, it is important to explore the moral atmosphere surrounding these two liturgies. What atmosphere is the Novus Ordo contributing to? Another example: the Novus Ordo is flexible. It includes a variety of different options. Scan the General Instruction of the Roman Missal and you will find this pattern repeatedly: a certain norm is put forward but language like *should* is used and other options are given if the priest so chooses. Eucharistic Prayer I should be used on Sundays, but this is not so strict as to prevent a priest from using the other prayers. Scan the Book of Blessings and you will see the common phrase "these or similar words," strongly suggesting that the priest can ad lib his own prayer instead of the described blessing. Within the Mass itself, there is a greater variety of optional votive Masses. For instance, there are four Eucharistic prayers, and music can be present to practically any degree. The priest can choose the ferial readings of the day or can opt for the readings for the saint on many days. He can choose the short or the long form of the Gospel.

This variety comes at a great price. Christ lays down specific guidelines in the Gospels. He strives not to remove one iota from the Law and takes the moral teaching of the Old Testament to its logical conclusion, developing it and making it binding on his listeners. He is strict, more than we recognize at times. It makes sense that even if we had not been given a particular liturgical law, certain things allow us to worship God more effectively than others. What would give God more glory, singing "Let All Mortal Flesh Keep Silence" or singing "Blurred Lines?" One of these is more suitable to worship of God. But Christ did lay down specific guidelines, and his apostles were faithful to them. They instituted liturgical rites, and these rites developed under the guidance of the Holy Spirit. What began as a diversity of practices settled into a steady liturgical tradition that admitted new elements slowly and cautiously. There are diverse rites today, speaking to the diversity of cultures and the differing emphases each apostle placed in the liturgies they helped create. But within each rite there is the steady action of the Holy Spirit, ensuring that the rite is always faithful to the Lord's commands and always serves as the best channel of his grace. A hasty development that ignored centuries of careful listening to the Spirit was unheard of.

Furthermore, the possibility of choosing between so many options introduced an all too human element into the Mass. The liturgy used to take its cues from God, but with the Novus Ordo, we have structurally oriented things so that it takes its cues from man. Who determines which prayers, readings, and songs the priest will use? The priest himself. Even if he does so for pious reasons, they will be *his* reasons. A priest may choose to use the Roman Canon and make the Novus Ordo look as much like the Latin Mass as possible because he knows that it is more in line with what God has asked of us. Still, this does not change the fact that because of the Novus Ordo this was *his* choice to make. He could manipulate the liturgy.

This focus on man comes back in *versus populum* when the priest faces the people. I have often been to a Novus Ordo liturgy, even before I had heard of the Latin Mass, and wondered to whom the priest was talking. The Eucharistic Prayer is obviously addressed to God, so why is the priest looking at me? We are no longer all facing the same direction awaiting the return of Christ and solemnly focusing on the sacrifice at the altar. We are looking at each other. With that re-orientation comes a subtle shift in focus. Priests experience this. Many feel like they need to keep things interesting because they are constantly looking at and speaking to the congregation. Consequently, the focus suddenly shifts to man rather than to God and the re-presentation of Calvary in humble obedience to the Father. Yes, more depends on the personal qualities of the priest in the Novus Ordo than in the Latin Mass. Because the congregation faces the priest at the Novus Ordo liturgy, it gives an impression of a community gathering rather than a solemn ritual. The point here is not that every priest who celebrates the Novus Ordo means to imply these things. The ethos simply points to them more naturally.

This brings me to my final point: the Novus Ordo is simply imbalanced. The priorities are skewed—from the emphasis on community participation to the focus on the priest's choice. These are not bad things in themselves, but they are certainly not the point of the Sacrifice of the Mass. Calvary is not about community participation or man's choice. It is about God's limitless mercy coming upon his humble people who have prepared themselves to receive it. This imbalance and disorientation apply to the very structure of the Novus Ordo. Often the Liturgy of the Word competes with the Liturgy of the Eucharist. Because of the additional and longer readings and the increased emphasis on the homily, one can easily feel like they attended a lecture followed by a semi-connected community ceremony. The new lectionary was designed to cover more Scripture, but it fails to consider that Scripture is in the Mass to connect us to the sacrifice of Christ. It is meant to bring up the high points of the covenants between God and man and to insert us into the mystery through particularly significant moments. The Mass is not a Bible study or an academic endeavor, and it is not a lecture followed by a simple meal. It is a ritual, a sacrifice, an act of profound worship, and every element of the liturgy should reflect that. The Latin Mass focuses on the moment of consecration: everything cuts to silence in preparation for it, and the fanfare returns rejuvenated once it occurs. In the Novus Ordo, everything is so variable and pushed together that silence, song, and sacramentals barely have any room to emphasize what is most important in the Mass. The priorities are shifted, and like it or not, the "body language" of the Novus Ordo communicates that message. It is still a valid Mass, and Jesus does come to us there, but you might be even more receptive to his graces if the liturgy were even more beautiful and reverent.

There is much more that I could say. Instead of going into more academic arguments, I would like to extend an invitation. Look at my experience with an open mind. If you have not been to a Latin Mass, try it out. Its depth and beauty are tremendous, and it cannot be taken in all at once. You will see that something profound is happening, but it may take six months of consistent attendance for things to click. Give it a shot and take the handful of belligerent parishioners with a grain of salt. Many of the people who attend are kinder than you may expect. Remember, you do not have to follow along perfectly to actively participate. All I knew was the Novus Ordo, and it has taken me two years to be completely at home in the Latin Mass. But it was well worth it, and the journey has been amazing.

CHAPTER 3

A RETROGRADE'S FAITH

TIMOTHY GORDON *holds degrees in philosophy, literature, history, and law. He is the author of* Catholic Republic: Why America Will Perish Without Rome *(Sophia Institute Press, 2019),* Rules for Retrogrades *(TAN Books, 2020), and* The Case for Patriarchy *(Sophia Institute Press, 2021). The following interview contains his unique stance on the traditions of the Faith.*

* * *

Could you please describe your upbringing and family life?
I'm a cradle Catholic. And being a cradle Catholic in the '80s and '90s meant that there was a conspicuous lack of Tradition in my catechesis. Even though I was brought to Mass every week of my childhood—and despite the evangelical efforts of my parents on my behalf—my post conciliar education in the Faith suffered badly from the so-called "spirit of Vatican Two." Parents of kids my age had no clue in those days how bad our religious education was. Accordingly, in religion class at Catholic school and at Mass, my friends and brothers and I snickered ceaselessly at the campy way in which the Faith was presented to us. Bear in mind, my experience probably

represents an above-the-mean participation in the Faith for the typical Catholic family at the time.

And yet, it was still modernistic enough to turn me into a high-functioning agnostic by the fourth grade.

My dad was a scientist, and he came into the Faith on an intellectual basis around the same time I began having serious doubts (whereas my mom was a cradle Catholic). His claims that the Catholic version of monotheism made far and away the most sense stymied some of my burgeoning agnosticism. But I never had the opportunity to witness the sacramental efficacy of his newfound Faith in action, which wasn't his fault; this was mostly because the liturgy my family attended was just so *awful*. For instance, my dad and I acquired the habit of mocking together the banal, ridiculous music we heard on Sunday at Mass.

I simply could not believe that either of my parents took the liturgy seriously. But in their defense, they took it as seriously as our bishops and priests intimated they should. The merely suggested "hard sayings" of the Church began to seem to me as if they were intended for children and not for mature intellects: frequently at Church my parents and I would hear non-negotiable teachings eschewed (although we didn't realize the teachings were non-negotiable at the time). This assumption stemmed from my observations of adult interactions as they dialogued about the Faith in a casual manner before or after Church. As every traditionalist knows: *lex orandi, lex credendi*. Because of the terrible content of the liturgy and the lackadaisical nature of the adults present—especially the clerics—I began in middle school and early high school to confirm my own suspicions that Mass was for nothing more than indoctrination in childrearing and that adults were free to check out (which I mostly saw adults doing during the liturgy).

One red-letter date in my malformation occurred when my mom told me about the true source of the presents that I received "from Santa Claus" each Christmas. Naturally, I was devastated and scandalized. Moreover, from that time forward, I began to apply my resultant skepticism far too broadly. It was after this tearful realization of my young life that I began to figure that since Santa was not really making the rounds—notwithstanding the palliative narrative the adults in my life had told me— God and His worship—going to Church—must be fake also. The primary factor inviting my young mind to spuriously connect what I had been rightly told by otherwise mostly unknowledgeable adults about the divine Creator of the universe and that similar-seeming misinformation about apochryphal Santa: the irreverent Sunday Masses I'd seen adults halfheartedly celebrating all my life. Such Masses reminded me of the perfunctory way in which the Santa Claus custom was propagated in the popular culture. In my view, the haphazard approach by "normal adults" to Sunday Mass aped their halfhearted attempt to convince me of the Santa Claus narrative. In both cases, they failed to live up to that warrant which their narrative required. (I'd begun to question Santa because of obvious blunders and easily-avoidable contradictions made by adults speaking in my presence. They should have known better: either tell me the truth or more vigorously maintain the Santa narrative with greater precision!) If the Eucharist was truly the "source and summit" of everything important, why wouldn't all the adults I'd ever seen at Mass revere it with literally everything they had?

Think about it from my perspective: it was not altogether illogical to connect the spiritlessness of the adult approach to religion and to truth more broadly. In either case, I imagined that I had now glimpsed some sort of "insider secret" of the universe: adults profess convenient things they don't truly believe (which even now, I believe to be true far too much of the time!). And I had some evidence for that view, even if I misapplied the meaning of that evidence overbroadly.

The conceptual connection in my young mind sounds rather silly now that I've studied the great intellectual rigors of the one true Faith—which prove anything but superficial. But for the next decade or two, I literally took it for granted that if adults would labor to convince their kids that Santa delivers presents once per year, they would take greater—if only slightly—pains to convince themselves of the afterlife. There's a definite logic to what I was not yet identifying as the doubt-generating machine of the practice of bourgeois religion (and the bourgeois way of life in general). Call it "suburban lex orandi, lex credendi." On that creed, the only thing adults seem to throw themselves into with any true verve is the acquiring and maintaining of wealth and status.

As committed Catholics with a mature faith understand, real religion, the one true Faith, is not for the fainthearted denizens of the suburbs. Accordingly, I must stipulate that those who genuinely love the Mass and the truth don't count as "suburbanites" in my view, even if they happen to live there. (For the record, I still use the Santa narrative with my own kids, but I will be much more careful to explain the purpose of the narrative after they realize the truth, and my kids also see my deep reverence for the Eucharist, which I hadn't witnessed much at all as a kid myself.)

Anyway, I suppose I was a "traditionalist" from my youth, even when I did not yet believe in the precepts of Catholicism. As soon as I learned in middle school about the modernizing agenda of many of the prelates at Vatican II—before, during, and after the council—I mistrusted it. I did not understand the complexities involved by the interplay of the divine protection of ecumenical councils as it combined with twentieth-century human agency by churchmen seeking to harm the Church. As I got older, I came to blame what I generalized as "the council" for my lack of faith, a pitfall that many likeminded folks continue to do. In a broad sense, I wasn't wholly wrong. Obviously, I had to blame something for the dispiriting liturgical innovations to which I had been subjected. *And the council that claimed such innovations as its own was not an unreasonable referent, although the story is quite a bit more complex than that.* Even in the post conciliar Church, grace abounds and opportunities to share in it regularly present themselves to the attuned mind and heart. In this finer sense, I was not accurate when I blamed the council for my lack of faith.

In sum, my upbringing in the Faith prepared me to become an authentic appreciator of tradition later in life. Intellectually and liturgically, I was *always* a traditionalist in the sense that I always figured if religion were true, it should be practiced with as much beauty as a human being could muster. In this vein, I never had a honeymoon period with the "Pope John Paul II" Church in which I grew up. I never took seriously the campy 1970s and 1980s religion textbooks in school that looked and felt like coloring books. I always loathed my childhood parish's kitschy felt banners, postmodern architecture, and tacky hymns (which sounded like they'd been written by the Monkees). I *always* ridiculed the tackiness of the liturgies I grew up seeing (during literally every Sunday of my young life). My brothers and I would imitate the ninety-degree bend at the elbow and the wrist of the cantor, inviting the rest of the parish to sing along to his inane Monkees tune. What person in his right mind enjoys "sacred" music such as this? Evidently, all the middle-aged ladies I'd ever seen at Mass. That's who.

How did you come to the Catholic faith? Did you have a conversion to Catholicism, or have you always been a practicing Catholic?
My conversion—reversion, if you will—was like that of Saint Augustine, not Saint Paul. I mean that it was very gradual, not sudden. It was in high school that I had my first exposure to good philosophy: specifically that of Aristotle and Saint Thomas. For the first time since fourth grade, I *wanted* to believe in Catholicism again. But at that time, I simply could not reconcile the lack of sacramental discipline during Mass with the idea that Catholicism was real and needed to be taken seriously.

I began a long journey consisting of reading Aristotle

and St. Thomas throughout college and early graduate school. I slowly came to appreciate the intellectual justification for the Faith, as well as the contrasting fact that no such foundation existed for other religions. After my marriage, just before the promulgation of *Summorum Pontificum* in 2007, I began attending a Traditional Latin Mass. It was at a diocesan parish, which by all appearances yielded enthusiastically to the "spirit of Vatican Two." Yet, on account of one good, old priest named Msgr. Ralph Belluomini—who befriended my wife and me, privately teaching us Italian—this parish allowed the Latin Mass, which Msgr. Belluomini offered weekly. (It is possible that I am misremembering the chronology— and that I actually began attending Msgr. Belluomini's Latin Mass immediately after the motu proprio in 2007.)

Still, at this point, even after attending the Latin Mass—as I sojourned to Rome to get my doctorate in Thomism—my conversion remained strictly intellectual. That is, I did not yet possess supernatural faith. It was only through heartache during the events of my first daughter Abigail's birth in Rome (and ensuing early years) that the experience of supernatural faith would come to me at last.

Abigail was born a month premature, on Tiber Island in central Rome, after experiencing in utero brain hemorrhages and post-hemorrhagic hydrocephalus which caused clinical epilepsy and cerebral palsy. Because of Abigail's condition, I returned from Rome with my small family without the PhD I had traveled abroad in order to get.

I returned to LAX airport in November 2008 without

a terminal degree in philosophy or an academic career (or even a job), with a newborn neurosurgery patient and a stalwart and lovely wife, with a few hundred dollars to my name, and with nerves jangled ostensibly beyond repair forevermore. I felt like Edmond Dantes returning to Marseilles an unrecognizably altered man from he who departed it.

Back in the States, while newly matriculating in law school, I developed a severe anxiety disorder, alongside post-traumatic stress disorder, as distraught as I was over young Abigail's ongoing condition. At the urging of Catholic author Michael O'Brien, I prayed specifically to the Holy Spirit—specifically for fortitude—for the first time in my life early in the morning on Holy Thursday 2011. Later that day, at evening Mass, two-year-old Abigail—who was at that point not yet capable of clear speech—began crisply whisper-chanting during the consecration of the Mass: "Holy Spirit . . . Holy Spirit." This was it for me. It was the most sublime thing ever to happen to me. On this side of the eschaton, I never assumed I would be one of the lucky few to have a breakthrough experience with the Lord as I lived and breathed. Yet in retrospect, it makes sense that it was my first daughter, Abigail—and this veritable miracle involved with her development—that finally won me over to the Faith. It was at this moment, of course, that my head and my heart united in faith, and I became fully Catholic.

Notably, I am always torn between characterizing my transition from my early experience of Catholicism to the fullness of the Faith as a "reversion," or more straightforwardly as a "conversion." In all earnestness, we lack the proper word to describe the transition from cafeteria Catholicism to authentic Catholicism, from cradle Catholic to tradition-loving Catholic. In retrospect, my embrace of the full Faith can only be described as part-reversion, part-conversion. Many likeminded Catholics of similar experience will find this compositional description satisfying: such an experience truly represents both *reversive* and *conversive* action by the soul.

What is liturgical abuse? What are some instances of liturgical abuse that you have experienced, and how can we help prevent these?
Far and away the most grave liturgical abuse imaginable is any single profanation—intentionally or incidentally—of the Eucharist, which occurs far too frequently each Sunday at most parishes around the world.

Aesthetically and intuitively speaking, the most egregious offense of all proves to be the new liturgical music. It represents perhaps an abusive interpretation of Vatican II's *Sacrosanctum Concilium* but all the more certainly an abuse of the human spirit and even the human ears! Even if you're not Catholic, if you're not hard of hearing, then you understand how the modern Catholic hymnal does not invite proper worship of God. The music contained in my childhood parish's "gather hymnals" coaxes faces to flush and off-key singers to join in. It is the most adulterated, tragically profane, hilariously unbeautiful music I've ever heard.

Following the scandalous implementation of the *Novus Ordo Missae* in 1969, one longs to "return to tradition" in 2021 by insisting upon an actual instantiation of the Mass described in *Sacrosanctum Concilium* (which would represent an organic development of the Traditional Latin Mass). Traditionalists must learn how important this next step in the "reform of the reform" will prove to be: neither *forgetting* nor *ignoring* but rather *reclaiming Sacrosanctum Concilium* from the radicals who commandeered and ignored it in the generation of the current iteration of the *Novus Ordo*.

As a conciliar document—and an authentic, ordinary act of the Magisterium—*Sacrosanctum Concilium* contains truths which are protected by the Holy Spirit. As a conciliar document, it also constitutes an integral part of our Tradition, even if we traditionalists have accustomed ourselves to deriding the documents of Vatican II as non-traditional. As a conciliar document, *Sacrosanctum Concilium* invites (or at least fails to preclude) a shockingly reverent liturgy, conceivably a barely modified form of the Traditional Latin Mass. Too many traditionalists forget that all conciliar documents constitute Tradition, and accordingly they speciously blame a rather defensible council document for the planned and codified heteropraxy of the most underhanded operatives at the council. What these traditionalists miss is that the Holy Spirit protected *Sacrosanctum Concilium* even from its own authors! We simply must pray for a faithful implementation of it.

If Pope Francis or any other post conciliar pope truly wants to guarantee and universalize Catholic faithfulness to the documents of Vatican II and its New Mass, then why are there so many members in the hierarchy who, in the pope's own name, oppose the replacement of the tacky disciplines (which are not in conformity with *Sacrosanctum Concilium*) in favor of more reverent ones (which are in conformity with *Sacrosanctum Concilium*)? This is the real question traditionalists should be asking. Too few ask it.

As Catholics, are we allowed to disagree with the pope? Or are we sinners if we disagree with *Laudato Si* and *Amoris Lætitia*?

It all depends upon the manner in which one interprets the word "disagree." Acts of the extraordinary Magisterium are always infallible. Conversely, the ordinary Magisterium is not infallible, yet demands obedience. Documents from the ordinary Magisterium (such as *Laudato Si*) can only become binding as a part of Tradition if they are habitually taught by later popes. Even though *Laudato Si* seems to be aligned with the United Nations Agenda 2030 and against Catholic social teaching, if five popes in one hundred years were to pick up on these ideas, then I don't see why it would not be considered a legitimate Magisterial document. We must wait and see if "ecological sins" (as framed in *Laudato*) prove to be a legitimate development of doctrine or merely an attempted novelty. I seriously doubt that the future Magisterium will habitually teach the new precepts in *Laudato*.

This line of reasoning does not apply for the document *Amoris Laetitia*, however (most specifically, its eighth chapter). The teaching of this chapter regarding divorced and civilly remarried Catholics contradicts two thousand years of Church teaching, not to mention the clear teaching of Christ in the Gospel. The principle of non-contradiction does not permit the ostensibly official interpretation of chapter 8 of *Amoris Laetitia* to be embraced by Catholics.[1] I'm not exactly sure how this squares with the function of the Magisterium, yet it will certainly be worked out in the future.

What are some of your favorite traditional devotions? What does your prayer life look like?
The Rosary: I try and pray five decades every day (with not infrequent failures—usually by falling asleep prior to completing five decades). Annually, I'm most committed to the practice during and immediately after Lent, during spring and summer. For whatever reason, each year, my devotion during the fall and winter months proves far more challenging, but I encourage everyone to try as hard as you can to do it every day, in accordance with our Lady's wishes.

In addition to our Lady, I am specially devoted to Her Most Blessed, Most Chaste Spouse, St. Joseph. As a father and husband, I pray to him, the Terror of Demons, for patriarchal charity and fortitude. I also frequently pray as a scholar to St. Thomas. Scholars need a conspicuous sort of audacity. A short prayer I pray before small or

---

1   The official teaching can be found in the document "Basic Criteria for The Application of The Chapter 8 of Amoris Laetitia." In the document, the pope ensures that there can be no other interpretation of the document other than the reality that persons living in an adulterous relationship can be permitted Communion.

large frightful life challenges is, "Jesus, Mary, and Joseph, be with us on the way." Also, I exhort Christians to have a look at *The Little Office of the Virgin Mary*, which is a microscopic version of the breviary. I try to pray "Saint Michael the Archangel" every night before bed, and for the souls of the faithful departed before each meal.

Finally, the natural and supernatural virtue of fasting cannot be overstated. My wife and I intermittently fast during Lent and throughout the year. It bulwarks our prayer lives in ways that other devotional practices seem impotent to do.

As a postscript to all of the above, I want to challenge everyone reading this book who attends the *Novus Ordo* Mass: kneel for Communion (even if your parish does not provide an altar rail) and receive the Eucharist on the mouth rather than on the hand. Strongly encourage your kids to do so as well.

Why do you think traditional Catholicism is growing, especially among young people?
The repopularization of the Traditional Latin Mass is inarguably responsible for the "Catholic spring" among faithful Catholic youth in America, for the reasons I've catalogued throughout this interview. In a word, young people keenly associate authentic religiosity with Tradition rather than novelty, and with somber quietude rather than tacky or voluble participationism.

If you could change one thing about the traditionalist movement, what would it be and why?

The primary setback to the culture of American traditionalism—which setback has little or nothing to do with Catholic Tradition itself—is that today's traditionalists incline strongly toward a neverending series of (what Milo Yiannopoulos calls) "purity spirals." Purity spiralling involves a puerile form of one-upmanship wherein two priggish Catholics in dialogue accelerate more and more rapidly toward moral absurdity, by rejecting (or claiming to reject) harmless or venial features of secular life: "Oh, your wife wears a bathing suit at the beach? Well, mine wears shorts and a T-shirt for reasons of modesty and purity." "No, she quit bathing suits last year and now wears a full-body bathing burqa as she floats virtuously in the sea."

True Catholicism and its moral teaching precludes recourse to purity spirals, since such exercises in phoniness prove to be performed repudiations of our active obedience before Christ's admonition to live "in but not of" the world. We Catholics are not called to hate our bodies or our corporeal existence in the fashion of Protestants, Gnostics, or Manicheans but rather to strive for natural (and supernatural) excellence. Just as grace builds upon nature, supernatural excellence builds upon natural excellence; many traditionalists seem to forget as much.

After all, our bodies comprise precisely half of what make us persons (along with our souls): accordingly, we should embrace the opportunities at physical excellence with which corporeal existence presents us. If we do so, we will come to find that we have begun to master moral excellence as well. The two cannot be separated in the fashion of the Manicheans.

Christ calls us to be worldly in the sense of virtuously mastering corporeal life here, without becoming morally corrupt (viz. being "of the world"). In still other words, Catholics should be good at even secular skills, hobbies, and crafts in the name of perfecting one's identity for heaven.

Instead, too many traditionalists in 2021 flirt with a form of "Catholic Puritanism"—a contradiction in terms—which rejects natural virtue supposedly in the name of supernatural virtue. They fail to realize that there is no shortcut to supernatural virtue which bypasses basic natural virtues such as amicability, pride in one's healthful physical appearance, athleticism, humor, as well as secular hobbies which do not directly involve our Faith.

Perhaps the most egregious offense against natural virtue among contemporary traditionalism is the strain of anti-intellectualism abiding therein. As yet another strain of "Catholic Puritanism," many traditionalists mistrust all—even healthy—aspects of the intellectual life outside the Church. As a result, one finds surprisingly bald errors in basic critical reasoning—popular tropes within traditionalist circles which don't square with plain *recto ratio*; for example, monarchy is regularly hailed by traditionalists as the "only" fully legitimate regime in secular politics, although many traditionalists struggle to embrace the *actual* monarchical descriptions of papal power described in Vatican One's document *Pastor Aeternis*. Too many trads have absolutized the liturgical disciplines we love (which are not absolute, and are thus subject to change) and relativized Catholic doctrines which are actually absolute (such as the sometimes inconvenient teaching on the pope's plenary powers described above).

It's not necessarily the fault of the traditionalist movement that this lesson in life balance (i.e., temperance and prudence) has mostly failed to transmit. Most of our prelates have failed us. We are "parish orphans." Like the eldest brother vying unsuccessfully to run the family in the stead of the home's absconded father, the traditionalist lay leader has done his best to sermonize his brothers, but without the benefit of the father's office or insight. Squabbling therefore breaks out constantly among the younger brothers. In this fatherless shadow, traditionalists are constantly jockeying for position. (Think of the apostles, who argued about the identity of Christ's best disciple even before Christ had left their side.) Until we somehow change this counterproductive habit, it will be impossible to feel truly at home among the denizens of the Traditional Latin Mass.

Tell us about any upcoming projects or events that you are working on:
In late 2021, my third book, *The Case for Patriarchy* (Sophia Institute Press, 2021), hit the market. The previous year, the good folks here at TAN published my second book, *Rules for Retrogrades* (TAN Books, 2020). You can check out more of my work by watching my podcast on YouTube, *Rules for Retrogrades*, and by reading my first book, *Catholic Republic: Why America Will Perish Without Rome* (Sophia Institute Press, 2019).

CHAPTER 4

A GOOD WORTH FIGHTING FOR

MY NAME is Stefanie Lozinski; I'm a writer, a mother, a millennial, and an unapologetic Catholic traditionalist.

As the frigid early days of 2018 dawned, I was twenty-five years old, and Catholicism was the only religion that I had not yet considered, the only worldview, really—God, or gods, or an empty eternity. I had explored pretty much all my options to varying degrees. The only version of me that I had not yet attempted to become was Catholic. Eventually, there's no rebellion left but to stop watching pornography, start wearing modest skirts, and to go to Mass on Sundays! If you seek the truth without ceasing, and you're honest with yourself, you will end up in the Catholic Church sooner or later, by the grace of God. And, I would add, if you seek the totality of Catholic truth, you will find the totality of Catholic praxis—traditional catechesis, traditional devotions, and especially the traditional liturgy.

I found myself alone in a hotel room in Dallas, Texas, singing *Dirt Road Prayer* by Lauren Alaina (I have a video of this very moment, and I cherish it) and praying to our Father in heaven for the first time in a very long while. I had spent the week prior at an intensive training course where I had been invited to learn about the Muslim Brotherhood, jihad, and the Islamic religion in general. It was a secular course; I arrived as a nominal Christian living a totally secular life, but something happened to me there, and when I left, I realized that my life would never be the same again.

Let's back up a little. It is the all-knowing, all-seeing Holy Spirit who converts us, and he began to work on me long before the come-to-Jesus moment I experienced on that trip. I was born in 1992 and baptized in the Eastern Orthodox Church as an infant. My father was (and remains) a very devout Greek Orthodox subdeacon, and my now-secular mother was far more religious when I was a young child. Along with my two sisters, we lived in a converted one-room schoolhouse in the country, where I was homeschooled for nearly the entirety of my education. I grew up going to the beautiful, reverent Divine Liturgy of Saint John Chrysostom every Sunday, and my father worked hard to teach me the Orthodox faith to the best of his ability. I knew about the Real Presence of Christ in the Eucharist. I knew about the saints. I knew about the *Theotokos*—the Blessed Virgin Mary, Mother of God.

Despite these gifts, there was something missing. I look back at that time of my life and I can see that I never really got it. I always felt like there was a wall between God and me even at those times in my life when all I wanted was the sort of faith that seemed to come so naturally to my dad. A big part of this was caused by two major problems in the Greek Orthodox parish I grew up in: an inordinate focus on Greek ethnicity at the expense of catholicity and a lack of catechesis and community. To this day, I often remind traditional Catholics that although good liturgy is necessary (and make no mistake: I'm very passionate about the Latin Mass), good liturgy by itself is not enough to keep people in the faith.

Around the age of fourteen, I ended up meeting some Protestant teenagers my age and joining their weekly youth group. I was desperate for connection. I never really had even one Orthodox friend, and it was very isolating, especially as my mother fell further and further away from the faith as I got older. This group of Protestants became some of my closest friends, and in turn, I became more and more involved in their version of Christianity. I spent more and more Sundays at their nondenominational worship services. It blew my mind that anyone wouldn't want to go to church if all it consisted of was a Sunday morning concert! Despite never fully accepting basic beliefs such as Sola Scriptura,[1] I see how much my thinking was influenced. At that time, I wanted to save my virginity for marriage, as did many of my friends. However, as time went on, I realized just how much the "anything but" culture was alive and well. I realized how few absolute moral standards there were, especially seeing that there was no confession or Holy Communion to worry about.

I was no better than my peers regarding my moral behavior, but the hypocrisy of the Protestantism I had never really embraced was what really bothered me. I wasn't sure what I thought about hell and judgment at

---

[1] For those unfamiliar, this is the Protestant belief in "Scripture alone" being sufficient for salvation.

the time, but I was sure that "say you believe in Jesus and you're saved" was a foolish way to look at things!

Within a year or two, I had begun dating an atheist boy I met at work. I stopped going to even nondenominational Sunday services. I disconnected more and more from my Protestant friends. My healthy, feminine desire to be cherished and protected and loved was easily warped into an acceptance of men who did not have my soul in mind, and sins against chastity further darkened my intellect. I didn't become an atheist at this point. Instead, I became a Wiccan! I experimented with tarot cards, Ouija boards, candle magic, and the like. I had some very frightening experiences with these things. They are not of God, and they are not harmless! I explored various religions throughout my later teen years, particularly those from the Eastern part of the world, infected as I was with the typical ungrateful attitude toward anything related to Western civilization. In 2015, in my early twenties, I was blessed with a son. No longer could I just do whatever I wanted—I owed it to both of us to figure out the direction I wanted my life to take.

During the election of Donald Trump, in the fall of 2016, I got my start as a writer and commentator. I built a following on Twitter, got paid pennies to write articles for independent news websites, started a YouTube interview show, and within a year, I found the news story that would eventually lead me to that fateful week in Dallas, and ultimately to the Catholic Church. A Canadian member of parliament named Iqra Khalid had put forward an anti-Islamophobia motion, and I discovered that she and her family had very sketchy ties to the Muslim Brotherhood. Most importantly, she was the president of the York University Muslim Student's Association (a Muslim Brotherhood front organization) in 2007. I found unassailable evidence that in 2014, this same Muslim student association was handing out literature at the university that defended wife beating and honor killings.

My work in political writing had led me to see the utility of Western religion in questions of governance, and my study of Islamic jihad had forced me to acknowledge moral questions I had long ignored. Some part of me wanted to know the right things to believe and the right way to live, as I had always had a passion for truth and had always believed one truth must exist, but the will to find this truth was stifled by the sinful life I was living.

My Islam-related work was getting a fair bit of attention at this point, and to my great excitement, I was invited to study the topic more deeply with other like-minded individuals. After a month of intensive reading and studying in preparation for my course, I packed my bags and flew to Dallas. We were driven to a secret location for security reasons, and I met the group I would be living and training with for the next week. We always began our long study days with a morning prayer, and three of the trainers would always make the sign of the cross before we ate. I found these things comforting, reminding me of childhood prayers with my dad, but I wasn't yet ready to accept the truths behind the piety.

A few days into the course, we were shown incredibly graphic videos depicting the reality of Sharia enforcement and jihad warfare. It must have been only fifteen minutes or so, but it felt like the horrific images dragged on for hours. Men hung upside down like animals in a slaughterhouse, their throats cut, blood running through troughs in the floor, fear and resignation in their eyes as they met their end; these were things I never imagined I'd see, but I know why they showed this barbarity. It was a reminder to us that we must tell the truth, without fear, even if people hated us for it—real human lives (and, more importantly, souls) depend on it.

Another video appeared on screen: a black girl in a long blue robe and headscarf, a little thing, probably under the age of fourteen. She was buried up to her chest in dirt and gravel, surrounded by men. They picked up stones. They threw them at her. I was already crying by this point. And then, she cried for her mother. The image of this little Muslim girl, crying, begging for her mom to help as grown men stoned her to death was horrifying. I watched the life leave her body, thousands of miles and who knows how many years away. I was helpless. Something broke inside me. I sobbed uncontrollably as the screen went blank, new friends at my side trying to comfort me. I felt as though my soul was rendered in two, if such a thing were possible.

I realized two things that day. I learned that true, deep, hateful evil exists. And I learned that though I hated evil and wanted to fight it, I had nothing to live for. The Christians who surrounded me, on the other hand, had hope. They looked at the relentless machinations of various Islamic jihad factions, the dire Muslim immigration situation in Europe, and the sheer magnitude of the task of "reforming" Islam and they knew that in the end, we would win. We would win because God would win. Thoughts of that young lady crying out for her mother stayed with me as the course ended. I couldn't shake her. I knew I had to stop being a coward and reach out for the truth in earnest. So I prayed, and the next day, I flew home. I texted my father on Saturday asking if he could pick me up for church the next morning. He was surprised and happy, but it was not to be. Freezing rain had come in the night, turning the country roads near my family's house to glare ice. He called me around nine, apologetic, promising to take me the next week.

I hung up, looked over at my two-year-old son and knew that I had to see God that day. The Orthodox parish was too far away. Though I had been unsure if I would return to Orthodoxy, I knew that I would not look to Protestantism. I knew I wanted to be near our Eucharistic Lord. We bundled up, went out into the cold, and walked up the street to the Catholic Church we had lived almost next door to for several years. It was a very modern, glassy sort of place, the style of architecture I would have disdained even before I discovered tradition! Never had I imagined I would ever cross the threshold of that church, but cross I did, wild toddler in tow. I started to cry in the narthex. He was there in the Blessed Sacrament. I knew it with certainty. The faith I had longed for as a little girl had finally been given to me.

From there, other pieces began to fall into place very quickly. Within a week, I had talked to the priest at that parish and told him I was interested in converting to Catholicism and having my little boy baptized. Since I was raised Orthodox, I had already received the sacraments, so I never had to attend RCIA classes. At the Easter Vigil, I did my profession of faith, and my son received the sacrament of Baptism. We were home.

Sanctifying grace is a very real thing. After I confessed over a decade of sins and began to truly amend my life, I felt the fog that clouded my intellect begin to lift. Christ's love was transforming me from the inside out in so many ways, but that lifting fog was what I most noticed. My thirst for truth was only beginning to be sated, and now, I had the will to pursue it further. I had already known a little bit about the new Mass and Vatican II even before I converted, thanks to my dad, but it didn't take me long to realize how rotten things were in the human element of the modern-day Catholic Church.

The Novus Ordo Mass was very strange to me. It had the Eucharist, but our Lord was not treated with the reverence I was used to growing up. I received on my hands out of fear of standing out, but it always felt wrong. The music was like a folky knock-off of the nondenominational Protestant concerts I had grown accustomed to as a teenager. Unlike so many "converts" to tradition, I had little time to grow a solid attachment to the Mass of Paul VI. My only real hang-up was the vernacular, which is quite understandable: I grew up in a community that so often put the Greek language over everything else.

However, despite this, I was very interested in the Latin Mass. I attended my first one with my father in Allentown, Pennsylvania, at a parish run by the Priestly Fraternity of Saint Peter. It was an early morning Low Mass, and it was absolutely beautiful. There was a sense of familiarity with the Divine Liturgy. It was very clear to me that East and the traditional West were closely related, whereas the Novus Ordo felt more like a cousin you see a few times a year.

Though I love the High Mass, I think the simple Low Mass will always have a very special place in my heart. Kneeling before the altar, eyes lifted to the elevated Host, it is made clear that we have an innate need for silence in our chaotic world. This peace has been a source of great healing for me, particularly from the evil things I have seen. Though I will never forget that Muslim girl, her blue garments, or her cries, God continues to fill my heart with images of hope. Her suffering was not mean- ingless. Her suffering may have saved my life.

Though I still attended the Novus Ordo Mass every day (I did not realize at the time that there was a Sunday Latin Mass relatively close by), it was a very short time before I began to consider myself a traditional Catholic. The more I let go of my past life, the more the unchang- ing teachings and traditional practices of the Church appealed to me. I started veiling at Mass, dressing more modestly, and receiving the Eucharist on the tongue. The more I learned, the more I became passionate about sharing the Faith with others. It was frightening to let go of the secular "brand" I had built for myself as a com- mentator, but I knew that I wanted to write what I was truly passionate about. I became a contributor to *OnePe- terFive* and *Catholic Family News*, where I still write to this day.

I went through a lot of difficult seasons since becom- ing Catholic, the sorts of things I don't believe I could have handled without the grace of God. Through it all, one thing has remained a constant gift. I have prayed the Rosary every day since about a week after I attended Mass for the first time.

Today, I am overjoyed that my son is being raised attending the Latin Mass every Sunday and holy day. Despite a couple of horrible heartbreaks and with the help of much prayer, I am engaged to be married to a wonderful traditional Catholic convert who loves Jesus and Mary as much as I do. I have a beautiful life, doing work I love from home and engaging my passion for learning every day. The beauties of the Catholic Church are so deep. I know I will never know everything there is to learn, and that thought fills me with joy. Most of all, I trust in God's love for us all, and I long for others to know him and to love him in return. After a life adrift, I have found truth, beauty, and goodness. I have found something worth living for.

CHAPTER 5

FROM SECULAR TO TRAD

STEPHANIE GORDON *is the wife of Timothy Gordon, who was featured in chapter 3. She has six children, runs her own YouTube channel, and has been featured in* Church Militant. *You can hear more from Stephanie Gordon by reading her upcoming book on Catholic femininity as well as her published articles.*

* * *

Could you please describe your upbringing and family life?
My upbringing was anything but ordinary for a traditionalist Catholic. My mom and dad met when they were in their teens. One thing led to another and my mother was pregnant with me when she was sixteen years old. My father's family is Mexican but were largely only Catholic by name and culture. He was expected (and forced) to marry my mother by his parents, and I could tell that his heart was never dedicated to the marriage. Dad was in the army, and so we were constantly in a state of flux. Consequently, he was often not present to my mother and me. Eventually, they got divorced, and I was raised by my mother.

My mother is devoutly pro-life, and she never once considered getting an abortion. But she was also an adamant liberal atheist, not even a "creaster" Catholic (someone who attends Mass only on Christmas and Easter). I only went to church when I was seventeen to eighteen years old with my father and his family. My dad settled in Orange County, California, and going to Mass was something we would force in between fun events like going to Disney World and amusement parks.

How did you come to the Catholic faith?
I am not going to lie; I had a very tumultuous and rough childhood. I was spiritual but not religious. I always felt something or someone was guiding me to do the right thing, despite the numerous bad examples and influences in my life. It was only after I met Tim that things started to turn around for my life religiously. When I was seventeen, I was dating Tim's best friend, but as I hung out with Tim, I found that I was more of a match with him than his best friend!

Tim was the first moral, intelligent, and well-structured man I had ever met. It is important to keep in mind that I came from a divorced family with no licit Catholic relationship; my whole life I grew up in an environment of fluctuation and no religion, just chaos! Even his half-empty Catholicism was balanced, structured, and moral from the perspective of a secular-atheistic background. I was always an old soul, and Tim's lifestyle called to my innate desire for ancient and foundational beauty. Tim let me know about the feelings he had for me in Dallas, Texas, while we were both in college. Nothing materialized, however, until we both left college and moved back to California to be with our families, and then we started dating!

My mother helped me find a man like Tim. Even though we disagree about everything, she was my biggest cheerleader. She helped me with my relationship with Tim and supported me 100 percent. Even though I was not even questioning being with Tim, she said I would be an idiot if I didn't pursue Tim back; she thought he was in a league of his own. It was through his influence that I rejected the secular worldview I was raised in. By God's grace, I was able to avoid a teenage pregnancy and the statistical likelihood given my own circumstances of being raised in a single parent home. And now, thank God, I am Catholic!

As a Catholic, did you have a transition from being a conservative Novus Ordo advocate to favoring aspects of traditional Catholicism? If so, what was your "trad-pill" moment or moments?

I think I have a unique perspective from anyone else in this book. I came into the Novus Ordo as a secular-atheist and knew nothing about Christianity, Catholicism, or theology. The other important aspect of my life to keep in mind is that Tim and I parody everything. Including our Christmas letters, we make fun of ourselves and the stupid decisions we made in the past year. When I first started attending the Novus Ordo, it should come as no surprise that I would make fun of the songs, tambourines, felt banners, and the "resurrecifixes." I thought that the liturgy was just a bad source of entertainment, a gathering.

My tradpill moment was not anything special; it just came from comparing the unstructured Novus Ordo to the well-structured and serious Traditional Latin Mass. All my critiques of the Novus Ordo were answered by the traditional Mass. I thought I was being clever by making jokes in my head about the Novus Ordo, but when I attended the traditional Mass, I realized that I was not unique: there was an entire group of people who thought the same exact way as I did about the new Mass and therefore preferred the strict rubrics of the old liturgy.

It was then that Tim and I started to realize that someone had to have purposely parodied the traditional Mass with the Novus Ordo. I was not able to understand that the liturgy was transporting me back to the intense suffering of our Lord, to the immense weight of our Lady at the foot of the cross, and that I was present at the sacrifice of our Lord when I attended the Novus Ordo. How could these overtly intense and profound themes be replaced by *On Eagles Wings* and *Gather Us In*? When I attended the traditional Mass, I finally found the liturgical roots and foundation I had been striving for since my chaotic and unstable childhood. When I met Tim, I realized naturally what a man should be. When I went to the traditional Mass, I naturally realized what a liturgy should be.

I have never felt the same kind of weight and understanding of sacrifice when I attend the Novus Ordo. I have had so much immense suffering in my life, and when I am at the traditional Mass, I find the purpose and meaning of my suffering. I feel united to our Lady at the foot of the cross. I understand the nature of sacrifice and how I can unite my own suffering with that of Christ's. When I started going to the traditional Mass, I no longer viewed the liturgy as a gathering or entertainment but first and foremost as a sacrifice, and I dared not crack any jokes. When I was at the Novus Ordo as a new Catholic, I understood that Jesus died for us as a community. But when I am at the traditional Mass, I understand that he died and suffered for *my* individual sins, as well as the sins of the world, and invites me to unite the sacrifices of my past to his cross.

What is liturgical abuse? What are some instances of liturgical abuse that you have experienced, and how can we help prevent these?

We go to the Novus Ordo because it's the closest and most convenient when the TLM is not being offered. One of the worst cases of liturgical abuse occurred when I was attending the Novus Ordo. If I am on Church grounds, I am veiling. I walked up to Communion, knelt, and went to receive Communion. In the presence of this veiled, knee-bent, authentically Catholic mother, the priest just shook his head at me. I audibly asked, "What?" He again shook his head. Confused, I stood up, and the priest said no to me as I stuck my tongue out even further. I was denied receiving on the tongue because it was *flu season*. I talked to Tim about the event afterwards; he was in the back with Abigail because she was in a wheelchair. When he heard what happened, he was horrified. Tim went and confronted the priest after the Mass, but he said, "Go and find another parish if you are not happy about it."

This was a big mistake. Tim looked him dead in the eye and said, "I am going to come into your Communion line next weekend, and you are going to give my wife and I Communion on the tongue because it is our right as Catholics to receive Communion on the tongue. Your boss says so."[1] The next weekend, the priest accepted that he was wrong, gave Tim, all his students, and me Communion on the tongue as we knelt.

Another horror story happened once my dad reconnected to the Catholic faith after he received an annulment. He lives in Utah now, and I went to visit him. He is in the middle of Mormon country, and we went into the new Catholic parish (which looks like a renovated pizza hut).[2] In the middle of Mass, a German shepherd ran down the aisle of the church. I asked a parishioner what was going on and she said, "Oh, that's Father B's dog! Isn't he so cute?" When I reacted with repulsion and disgust, people began getting upset *at me* for acting bewildered. After this buffoonery, I kid you not, a nun got up to read and she was wearing a tie-dyed shirt with a cat's face in the dead center of the shirt—not a habit, but a tie-dye cat shirt.

I tried my best to be reverent and prayerful during the

---

[1]   See *General Instruction of the Roman Missal*; Appendix for the United States, 240b.

[2]   Stephanie Gordon, "Was That Altar Dog Properly Trained?," *Church Militant*, May 5, 2018, https://www.churchmilitant.com/news/article/was-that-altar-dog-properly-trained.

Mass, wondering what sort of nightmare I had found myself in. After the Mass, my father excitedly introduced me to Father B. The priest, wearing a hoop earring, came up to meet me after Mass, and he grimaced at me. I wondered why he was grimacing, and it was because of my *veil*. I was grimacing at the liturgical abuse; he was grimacing at my traditional reverent devotion. In both cases, these priests discouraged and were repulsed by traditional devotions of our Faith in favor of newer additions to the liturgy. Unfortunately, I am sure many of the readers can relate to these two cases of liturgical abuse.

As a teacher, my female students often ask me about traditional aspects of the Faith and how they seem sexist, including women veiling and the entire virtue of modesty. How would you respond to these claims of sexism? What this boils down to is this: women think they know better than the God who created them. They think they personally know better their role in society, the family, and the universe than the Creator of the universe. Catholics do things all the time to show that they are set apart from the world. When I go to Mass and wear a veil on my head, I tell the world I am subject to God and I am subject to my husband as the head of the family. I am the woman, and I am the heart of the family. I do many things that my husband could never do, including *birthing children*. While I could try and be more like my husband, I need to accept and surrender that it would go against my nature. It is more like the Virgin Mary to be submissive to God and my husband. Wanting to smash patriarchy is the total opposite of the Virgin Mary. Mary is the woman we should emulate. She is the Mother of God, the mother of us all. Women, at the end of the day, should emulate the ideal woman. Just like men should emulate the ideal man, Jesus Christ.

It is very important for young Catholic women to understand that they need to find a good Catholic husband. I am so sick of hearing women complain about how their husbands are idiots. You chose him! Husbands have the most difficult job, in my opinion. Having the husband be the head does not make me a slave; it is freeing. The chaos and disorder of our society is rooted in destroying the understanding of the woman being the heart and the man being the head of the family. Women who do not submit themselves to a husband who loves them live a life of chaos, disorder, and sin. It is a beautiful and wonderful thing to submit yourself to a man who would die to protect you. I must be the Virgin Mary for my husband and my children. He must be the Christ of the family for myself and my children.

What kind of men do we want for society? Can a company run properly with multiple CEOs? There can only be one head for one body. If we are not preparing our men to be the heads, what kind of men are they going to be?

What are some of your favorite traditional devotions? What does your prayer life look like?
My favorite saint to pray to is Our Lady of Sorrows. The suffering of our Lady is such an amazing mystery to

ponder. We also have had such profound suffering in our married life, and she has helped us through it all. Saint Michael the Archangel Prayer is the first prayer I pray every day. I also highly recommend the Consecration to Mary through the method of St. Louis de Montfort.

Why do you think traditional Catholicism is growing, especially among young people?
People are striving for truth; they are repulsed by how gross and ugly our culture is. There was something in the Church before Vatican II that was wholesome, true, and good. Millennials who are not secular don't want a watered-down version; they want the whole truth! They need an anchor for the crazy world we live in nowadays. We do not need priests who rap, play guitars, or ride hoverboards. We need real, true priests, warriors for Christ!

I met a priest named Father Ralph Belluomini and he taught Tim and me Italian. I kept saying something in Italian wrong, and he just abruptly said to me, "What are you stupid? Do it properly!" This is what we need in the Church. We need strict and stern priests who speak the truth and will not cave to error.

If you could change one thing about the traditionalist movement, what would it be and why?
Traditional women do not have to be frumpy to be traditional. You do not have to wear gunnysacks. You can still be beautiful and be traditional! I get judged for looking nice and having style while going to Mass. There is this

idea that any flashy, extravagant, or style is anti-feminine. This is just so backwards! You can still look nice without being prideful or vain.

I also think makeup is not intrinsically evil. I have met many traditionalist women who think that you must be a plain jane to be a true woman. This is backwards in the traditional movement! It is important for men and women to keep themselves in shape and look nice for their spouses, and there is nothing intrinsically wrong with makeup or dressing nicely. There must be a virtuous middle ground between not caring about your appearance and being extremely vain. I am not ashamed of liking makeup, clothes, and shoes. We are not puritans, we are Catholics!

Another thing is, I think too many traditionalists are just *nerds*. They can be like Ned Flanders from the Simpsons. We need red-blooded and passionate men and women in traditionalism. We need men that make time for boxing, wrestling, and weightlifting and women who care about how they look and express themselves. We need to be in the world, not of the world. And I feel like traditionalists often find themselves in neither camp. Many Novus Ordo Catholics are in the world and of the world, and traditionalists need to make sure they don't jump onto the other extreme of not being in the world or of the world.

CHAPTER 6

THE ARCHITECTURE OF BELIEF

Matthew Dom is a graduate from Franciscan University of Steubenville/Gannon University as a part of an engineering program. This chapter will reflect how the beauty of Churches should reflect the reality and transcendence of God rather than the immanent and disordered architecture of postmodernism.

* * *

I stood blinking in amazement at the enormous building that I was in. I stood astonished with admiration and no small amount of awe and reverence at this new building in which I had the blessing to attend Mass. It was breathtaking. The ceiling was higher up than I imagined any ceiling possibly could be. On the walls were fantastic decorations all running up to the ceiling, extending up to heaven and offering some sort of prayer bigger than the words my five-year-old vocabulary could explain. I wandered about with my mouth agape and my head turned back as I stared up into the lofty rafters of the overhanging roof. I looked at the stained-glass windows that depicted the lives of various saints and cast frantic little fractals of colored light down upon me in the pews. It was the first time I'd ever been to Saint Mary's in Woodstock, Illinois, which had just opened, and we had just attended the christening Mass. Never in my life had I imagined a building could be quite so awe-inspiring. I had seen other beautiful churches before, but they had not struck me in this same manner. After Mass, I would stand in the atrium of the church and stare at the awe-striking marble statue of Saint Michael the Archangel. This impressive statue towered over the serpentine Satan while he brandished a golden sword ready to plunge it into the fallen angel.

Before attending Saint Mary, our parish was Saint Margret Mary Church in Huntly, Illinois, where my father was the youth minister. After attending one of his high school talks despite being too young, I had a nagging question for him. "Is this really Jesus, and if he is really God and he really and literally resides in the tabernacle, why does the church look like this?" Saint Margret Mary Church looks almost like a large square tent, not to mention its enormous wood-paneled ceiling and rather bland altar. "Shouldn't the church look more like a castle since Jesus is a king?" I remember asking. My father explained to me that there are other churches, and some of them do. There is Saint Peter Basilica in Rome where the pope offered the sacrifice of the Mass, and it had some of the most beautiful artwork in the world. When we returned home, he showed me pictures of Saint Peter Basilica and told me about taking older kids in the youth group there for pilgrimages. Inspired by this, I asked, "Is it too expensive to do that here, and if not, *why not* do that here?"

Since then, I have seen what bringing Saint Peter's to the States looks like. I have had the fortune while growing up to participate in the Sacrifice of the Mass at beautiful churches. When I moved to the city of Milwaukee, Wisconsin, I had the opportunity to attend Mass at the Basilica of Saint Josaphat. This is one of the most beautiful churches in the United States, if not the most beautiful. And my response to even walking into the building was one of unworthiness and reverence and awe. This basilica was designed to be like a smaller version of the beautiful basilicas in Rome. It is glorious. But even that description is inadequate. I have the great blessing of God to be a parishioner at the basilica and to attend Mass there every day. Every surface depicts a scene from the Gospels or of a saint's life. And many separate times, when my irrevocably short attention span drifts during Mass, I have found myself staring at a depiction of one of the Gospels found on the wall. When I regain attention, I typically find out it is a scene from the very Gospel being read!

When your attention leaves the sacred act being committed in front of you (the Sacrifice of the Mass), you should find yourself focusing on the sacred images and statues surrounding you. These images allow you to quickly return your attention to the Mass at hand due to their depiction of the sacredness and beauty of the liturgy. The artwork depicting the lives of the saints ought to direct your attention to the highest point of the kingdom, which is the Holy Sacrifice of the Mass.

In the Midwest, there was a unique but not altogether unrecognizable architectural style present in the new churches in the late nineteenth and early twentieth centuries. The Polish cathedrals, as they came to be

known, were something taken out of the Old World.
They come from a place of both Eastern European and
Baroque style churches that were built by the new Polish immigrants quickly filling up the shores of the Great
Lakes. These cathedrals often took on the layout of many
older, more famous churches. Because of their relative
poverty, new and innovative building methods had to be
used. Things had to be made more cheaply, but they still
needed to hold their sacredness and beauty to praise the
Lord. Instead of using real marble, often painted stones
had to do the trick, and to great effect. Marble otherwise
unavailable in this region of the country could be used
in the church, but without the enormous costs. These
churches quickly sprung up in places like Chicago, Milwaukee, and Indianapolis. Just in the Chicago region
alone there are the basilicas of Saint John Cantius, Saint
Josaphat, Saint Stanislaus, and the National Shrine of
Mary Help of Christians at Holy Hill. Every one of
these churches remains breathtaking, and something
completely fresh, while remaining also something very
recognizable. And all receive praise from both Christians
and non-Christians for their beauty and timelessness.
They are places where the person can truly experience the
transcendent, places fitting for the Sacrifice of the Mass.

The Polish immigrants of Milwaukee had a problem. They wanted to build a house for the living God
to dwell—a place fitting to say Mass in. But they were a
relatively poor community and did not know how they
could afford the costs of a new building that would meet
their standards. By providence, the post office building in Chicago was closing. They needed more space

and would be moving to a far larger location (which is now also vacant). And they just so happened to have tons upon tons of marble and stone that made up the old post office. The parishioners pitched together to raise the funds and bought the building; now they had their stone, and then they needed to get it to Milwaukee. They carefully disassembled the old post office and pictured every block of stone. It was then carefully planned where it would go in the new structure. Each stone was loaded onto rail cars and shipped north. Each one was then carefully unloaded and laid in the streets to be assembled into part of the slowly growing basilica. Then painters were called in to paint enormous murals covering every surface with depictions of the lives of the saints and the actions of Christ in the Gospels. And the stones were painted over to look like marble so convincing that unless looked at closely with fine detail, one would never even surmise this fact.

While the post office might have been garish in its own time, it was disassembled carefully and reassembled lovingly into something altogether more beautiful, more sacred than what it had been before.

When I walk into the basilica, the beauty takes my breath away. My eyes, though they dart about, are cast down in shame in dismay at my meager raiment and state of mind. And yet my soul wishes to fly about, to be raised up into the apse of that beautiful building, dancing with the angels, who supposedly would be the only beings allowed there. My mind is lifted from its place of kneeling and thrown into the greater and vast world God has made, sent careening along a path insatiably until

I can find the origin of such a marvelous creation. The atmosphere of that place is intoxicating, it is uplifting, and quite literally, if I were to put it into the words of the critical theorists, oppressive. Hegemonic, hierarchical, it was totalizing. And it was good.

In the words of Dr. Jordan Peterson, who would oppose that description by the postmodernist, would say that it taps into some deep and ancient hierarchical idea present in the very depths of our consciousness. But he would be wrong. It is not something that simply exists in the tumultuous caverns underlying our psyche, but instead it is arrayed in all brilliance and splendor glittering in the sunlight and the colorful beams of light that come through its stained windows. There is literally a metaphysical affection upon the soul by the lofty arching of the church. It calls as if from a distant land, into our hearts beckoning us to our true home. It inspires us, as the Church Militant, to press on with depictions of those in the Church Triumphant. Beauty touches the soul and fortifies our reception of our Lord's body and blood, which makes us whole. The great cathedrals of the Middle Ages reflect this reality and were built for people seeking union with God. Quite simply, the whole medieval world was bigger than the world in which we currently live. They ambled attentively in the shadows of colossal Roman ruins and sang joyously in the painted light of nascent cathedral windows. While we, in our modern world, scurry nervously in the shadows of mirroring skyscrapers and tweet angrily in the portable light of mobile phones.

Since the very first time I heard the expression "form

follows function," it struck me as one of those ideological slogans that people share without caring about its meaning. Much like the silly claims that "we only use 10 percent of our brains" or that "you ought to question everything" or "the cold will make you sick," this claim about architecture and design is tossed out flippantly for the sake of conversation. But as a biomedical engineer, I have had to think about this epigram quite a lot. Is this *really* the way to do better design? I suppose when I design a better prosthetic limb, it is good to break it down into its most important components, those pieces that are most functional. This will make the device as simple as possible, with less chance of failure.

But is that really *the* guiding principle? It seems as though it is not. Even worse, this same mentality is applied to biology. When researching anything from neurology to adult stem cells, you will hear this phrase applied to how cells work. When questioned about form following function, some strange, irrational, and emotional response is frequently provided. But is that not how Aristotle and Saint Thomas Aquinas approached things? Didn't they look to the four causes?[1] They did. Is that the same as looking at something's function? No, it is not. Analyzing artifacts in this way yields a far richer understanding of the thing, and a far richer design.

The function of the thing compresses the whole process of thought into analysis of the final cause, what the thing is aimed at. It is the act of looking at how it is

---

1   Matter (what it's made of), form (its essence), efficient (who made it or how did it come to be), and final (purpose, goal).

used and making every part of that thing aim toward that function. This results in a shallow understanding, not considering the necessity of beauty, of transcendence, and of human reception. When ignoring the formal cause (the structure of a thing), the material cause (what a thing is made of), and the efficient cause (how that thing is made), *simplistic* and *uninhabitable* structures are produced. In the world of human life, there is a language of design that arises from our interaction with the world. The materials of building speak in unique ways: marble conveys reverence, gold speaks of royalty, granite of repose, wood of practical function. Additionally, the form of our structures communicates ideas and emotions. Archways recall the open airy vaults of the heavens, square rectilinear shapes describe strict attention and formality, and rounding areas invite ambulation along their borders. This is missed when the focus is simply on economically accomplishing the functional task at hand. Prayers are truncated and formality is removed for the sake of a thrifty progression of the task at hand. This is well suited to the lecture halls of computer programmers or engineers but inhospitable in the places of life and in the sanctuaries of worship.

Much of what is important about a building, or anything I have ever designed, is that it fits into its context. What a thing is must also fit with *where* it is and what it is *with*. There is some very important modesty in the thing, both on the inside and out. When a building is built, it must be seen in the context of where it exists: in a corn field, in a quaint brick adorned town, a busy city street. Many of the most beautiful churches across Europe fit very nicely as the crowning point of architecture for the rest of the city—as if all the buildings know their place, as homes to be lived in, as stores to be shopped in, and ultimately, the church to be worshiped in.

In their time and place, a church is literally the container of the Gospel, both as the Word of God and body of the Word made flesh. Even in the early days of Christianity, the Sacrifice of the Mass was celebrated in "remembrance of" him to whom all Christians gave their lives in their homes, at their tables, and in the catacombs in the tombs. It was literally where the Gospel took place in the lives of those who lived out their attendance of that celebration.

Before going much further, two questions must be asked: *What is the purpose of a church? Why do we build them?* Well, the church is the dwelling place of God. But for what end? Why would the eternal God of the universe, who is *Ipsum Esse*, the Act of To-Be, want to come to this small far-flung rock in this created universe? Because he loves us and wishes to "draw all things to [himself]" (Jn. 12:32) for our salvation. Much like the larger Church, which he forms and makes perfect for himself as his bride, so too do we form churches that are made perfect for us as we become his bride.

The churches are the place where, in the simple and mundane practice of our lives, we begin our entrance into the wedding feast of the Lamb. Like the Temple of Solomon or the synagogues, it combines two aspects of human spiritual life: a place to hear the Word of God and a place to be sanctified in the blood of the Lamb, the Word made flesh, who was slain for our offenses. They

are described as the Gospel in stone: "Be you also as living stones built up, a spiritual house" (1 Pt. 2:5). Those
churches fulfill the prophecy of Christ: "If these shall
hold their peace, the stones will cry out" (Lk. 19:40).
They are, just like the temple of Solomon, the dwelling
place of the Lord, and as such, they are a microcosm
of the universe. The world is seated and mirrored in the
temple. Churches contain the life of Christ, as they contain Christ himself.

This phrase—form follows function—is pertinent
because it has been a guiding principle of architecture
for almost a century, and for almost a century, it has
been *ruining* architecture. Buildings no longer fit into
their surroundings or even into their own facades. Each
new building is a flashy and notable thing that cries out
for attention for both building and architect. They are
a mere stopping point of interest along a tour and not
a place to arrive. They are not destinations to arrive at
because they are not buildings to *dwell in*. Instead of following the style of the buildings surrounding them, the
new structures built according the form from function
ideology make themselves as unique and novel as possible to bring in lavished praises. They collect praise but
do not give any. They stand as enormous concrete for-
tresses or as flamboyant shiny shards.[2] Those buildings
defy the common language of design and the humble
human understanding of structure. These designs seem

---

[2]   Two modern churches that match these criteria include Saint
       Mary of the Assumption in San Francisco and the Crystal
       Cathedral in Orange County, California.

awkward, like a gaudy teenager incapable of existing in his own skin, and much less in a room of other people. Buildings built in this way, while trying to emphasize their function, compress their existence past the point of even being *functional*. When the form follows the function, the function then is called into question; the function is now on the table, and off the altar.

When considering the context of the time, what is needed is not a throwing away of everything that has come before. In no way is that the case. What is needed is an understanding of the Gospel as it is lived in that time. It is the same Church from the moment it is born from the side of its Bridegroom, through persecutions, and through glorious assertion in the world, and even today as it is pushed into obscurity. "If any man among you seem to be wise in this world, let him become a fool, that he may be wise. For the wisdom of this world is foolishness with God" (1 Cor. 3:18–19). Lest the corruption creep in too quickly, we must not change with the times or not change at all; instead, we must be what changes the times.

We must approach the building of a sacred place for the dwelling of the Lord of Hosts with humility and reverence. The Temple of the Old Testament is the Temple of Solomon because God would not allow David to build it:

> Go, and say to my servant David: Thus saith the Lord: Shalt thou build me a house to dwell in? Whereas I have not dwelt in a house from the day that I brought the children of Israel out of the land of Egypt even to this day: but have walked in a tabernacle, and in a tent. In all the places that I have gone through with all the children

of Israel, did ever I speak a word to any one of the tribes of Israel, whom I commanded to feed my people Israel, saying: Why have you not built me a house of cedar? And now thus shalt thou speak to my servant David: Thus saith the Lord of hosts: a I took thee out of the pastures from following the sheep to be ruler over my people Israel: And I have been with thee wheresoever thou hast walked, and have slain all thy enemies from before thy face: and I have made thee a great man, like unto the name of the great ones that are on the earth. And I will appoint a place for my people Israel, and I will plant them, and they shall dwell therein, and shall be disturbed no more: neither shall the children of iniquity afflict them any more as they did before, From the day that I appointed judges over my people Israel: and I will give thee rest from all thy enemies. And the Lord foretelleth to thee, that the Lord will make thee a house. And when thy days shall be fulfilled, and thou shalt sleep with thy fathers, I will raise up thy seed after thee, which shall proceed out of thy bowels, and I will establish his kingdom. He shall build a house to my name, and I will establish the throne of his kingdom for ever. I will be to him a father, and he shall be to me a son: and if he commit any iniquity, I will correct him with the rod of men, and with the stripes of the children of men. But my mercy I will not take away from him, as I took it from Saul, whom I removed from before my face. And thy house shall be faithful, and thy kingdom for ever before thy face, and thy throne shall be firm for ever. (2 Sam. 7:5–16)

Catholics must recognize that it is God's prerogative to make us into his dwelling place. The architecture of our churches should reflect the tremendous quote from Saint Paul: "Know you not, that you are the temple of God, and that the Spirit of God dwelleth in you?" (1 Cor. 3:16).

The Bible is bracketed by the creation of the Church. The book of Genesis opens with the creation of a church—this world in which men live, "and it was good"—and ends with the book of Revelation, which tells of the creation of the new Church: the new heavens and the new earth, the Bride of Christ. And in this story from one church to one more perfect Church, we ourselves are fashioned to hold in us the Son of God. *Deus fit homo ut homo fieret Deus*, as the Church Fathers said (God became man, that man might become God). This is breathtaking, for we also are a temple to the Lord, and in our rejoicing with him in the Eucharist, in our bodies we hold the living God. As such, it is our duty to live our lives as gloriously as those churches whose splendor gives glory to God. Churches must be where we live well, where we worship well. The proper worship of God is the teleological end of man, our highest purpose and goal; this is the principle of our Faith. Therefore, the architecture of our churches must reflect the architecture of our Faith.

CHAPTER 7

TAKING THE PILL

"You could take the blue pill; you'll wake up in your bed and believe whatever you want to believe. Or you could take the red pill; you'll stay in Wonderland, and I'll show you how deep the rabbit hole really goes."

The above quote has been immortalized in the famous award-winning movie *The Matrix*. The term *red-pilled* has been popularized for various moments of an individual realizing the truth about a given circumstance and admitting that they previously held the wrong, but generally accepted, position on a topic (the blue-pilled position). The blue-pilled position within the Catholic world has been the belief that traditionalists are the weird, pale, and miserable individuals who hate the pope, live in bunkers, and cling to dead and outdated beliefs. While there are scandals in the Church, the future looks bright by encouraging new, progressive, and innovative practices into the liturgy, such as liturgical dancing, guitars, and charismatic renewal. Or so the story goes. In this account of my life, I will be presenting you with the pill that the millennial generation has consistently selected instead of the blue-pilled position: the tradpill. While you initially read through this conversion story, it is going to sound the same as all the generic witnesses you have heard in the past, but trust me, there is an important twist.

I suppose the best place to start is the beginning. My name is Kenneth Alexander. I am twenty-five years old. I grew up in Mont Vernon, New Hampshire. The town barely surpassed two thousand in total population, and the neighboring town of Amherst used to joke that we had more cows than people. I was blessed to grow up in a family of five with both my parents living under the same roof and they never got divorced. I also had two older sisters who were my first best friends, Rachel (who is one year older than me) and Kate (who is three years older than me). At the time, I did not realize how blessed I was to experience growing up with a relatively stable family life—it has become commonplace to grow up in a single parent household or with estranged siblings— and I thank God every day for the early childhood I experienced.

It was in this stable home that I was introduced to the foundations of the Faith. Every night before bed, my dad would read from *Aesop's Fables* and a Bible picture book, and he would ask us to tell him the moral of each story. We would attend Mass on Sundays at my local parish in Milford, New Hampshire, and on occasion, my mom would lead the Rosary as a family after dinner. Besides my parents' influence, my grandfather would also teach me the Faith using the Baltimore Catechism. At every family gathering, he would have all the cousins meet, and we would go through a chapter from the catechism and answer questions from quizzes he had made for us. Even though I pretended like I did not enjoy these lessons at the time, when I look back at my childhood, those are some of my fondest memories.

At first glance, it would seem like my childhood was relatively free from anything that would cause me to doubt my Faith, but looks can be deceiving. In first grade, I began attending public school, and for the first time in my life, I encountered people who did not believe in Jesus. And to make matters worse, they did not even believe in God. I remember the moment vividly: a girl in my class and I somehow got on the topic of creation during a kickball game. She confided in me that she did not believe that God created human beings but that we evolved from a chimpanzee (obviously, this is not literally what evolutionists believe, but give her a break, she was in first grade).

I could not understand what I was hearing. I had assumed everyone was at least raised to believe in Jesus or that there was a God, but I could not wrap my head around trying to live life without a notion of God. Over the course of my life, public school would introduce me to individuals who were far more advanced in their understanding of the world than I was. I quickly learned that I was very sheltered as a child, which I am mostly thankful for. Childhood innocence is a rare quality to have in the modern world, and I am very grateful to my parents for shielding me from the scandalous aspects of our culture. Nothing made me realize just how sheltered my Mont Vernon classmates and I were than the transition from Mont Vernon Village School (MVVS) into Amherst Middle School (AMS), in the next town over. It was at this school, as a mere seventh grader, that I encountered classmates who discussed pornography, premarital sex, underage drinking, and drugs, among other worldly vices. When my new Amherst friends would discuss some of these topics, I would always be the one who had to ask what on earth they were talking about, and they would always express their shock that I had not discussed these yet with anyone since they had learned about these vices back in fourth and fifth grades.

I now look back in horror at how exposed my seventh-grade classmates and I were! The Mont Vernon students went from one extreme of being largely sheltered at MVVS to the extreme of being exposed to nearly everything at AMS. As a teacher at an academy, I look at my seventh- and eighth-grade students for what they are: children. It makes me shudder with horror that the average public school student knows sexually explicit and other mature content at such young ages, and I can only imagine that the age for losing innocence has only decreased since the time I was in middle school. During my youth, I became heavily involved in sports, which allowed me to engage my peers.

Sports largely became a replacement for my faith. They gave my life direction and purpose, yes, but they also unfortunately made me think that the Faith was largely irrelevant for the life of a modern teenager. The Catholic beliefs I learned as a child appeared abstract and impractical in the life of a teenage athlete. Sadly, everyone I knew was committing what I was told were mortal sins daily and they did not appear to be hellbound; on the contrary, they were the ones who were popular, attractive, and funny.

On top of these doubts, I thought that going to Mass was extremely corny and effeminate. Listening to the music (which I thoroughly enjoyed as a young boy since the songs gave me positive emotions) became a cringe-inducing occasion. An older woman who cared deeply about the Faith but could not sing to save her life belted out psalms and hymns off key and pitch, much to the dismay of the attendees. Holding hands during the Our Father was one of my favorite moments as a child, but as I grew up, I realized that I merely enjoyed that experience because it resembled my kindergarten classroom. Every day during football season, I would do countless burpees, hundreds of push-ups, and punish my body with mental and physical discipline. But when I attended Mass, I felt like I was going to some poorly sung musical that was loose and undisciplined. Coincidentally, as I began having all these negative realizations about the liturgy, my family stopped attending Mass every Sunday.

I had largely abandoned the Faith in my adolescent years from middle school into high school. I began to date girls, drink underage, take drugs recreationally, view pornography indiscriminately, and I began acting on the passions that modern society told me were masculine. Sure, I still believed in God and I still thought religion was necessary for society. But the Church needed to change with the times; it needed to let loose and understand that modern man was not going to adhere to the ancient teachings on sin, especially not the sexual ones. Up until my sophomore year, I continued living this lifestyle without even contemplating my actions or their consequences. Without extraordinary grace acting in my life, I probably would have continued this lifestyle and maintained my cafeteria Catholicism until the present day. One of the greatest moments of grace that I received happened at a Thanksgiving party hosted at my cousin's house: I walked into the family party and I participated in the standard meet and greet small talk. But then something happened that would change my life: I saw my cousin Jake, who I had not seen since he left to study at Franciscan University of Steubenville, and he was different.

I could not put my finger on it, but now I realize that he had what I was seeking in all the wrong ways: he had happiness and authentic joy. I had encountered countless people who, for lack of a better word, were very fake. I am sure we have all encountered people like this in our lives. Fake people pretend to be happy and cheerful when certain people are around, but as soon as those certain people leave, they say every uncharitable insult they can about them. For those of you who know what I am talking about, I hope you get the opportunity to have an experience like the one I had with Jake that day, and I hope you know authentic joy when you see it. Jake and I sat down and talked for hours before the food was ready, took a break to eat, and then continued talking until the end of the party. I asked him questions about the Eucharist, confession, why only men can be priests, how it could be possible not to have sex or watch pornography, and nearly every other cliché anti-Catholic propaganda that I had heard during my public school education. He fielded every question with a smile, thoughtfully, and without any slight tone of disrespect.

Finally, at the end of the conversation, I asked him the question that was on my mind when I first saw him that day. The conversation went something like this:

"Jake, why are you so happy? Where does your joy come from? Everything you have described to me is so counterfactual to how nearly everyone else I have met lives. Yet, you are the only one who seems happy. Why is that?"

He sat and thought about the question, staring up at a spot on the ceiling, and I patiently waited to hear his answer. I could tell he was trying not to answer the question pridefully, or to step on my toes by being too blunt.

"I would say . . . that living out the Gospel, and most importantly receiving the sacraments, fills you with joy. It allows you to not merely live but to enjoy life. In fact, I think there is a Bible verse that discusses this. I might get it wrong, but it goes something like 'I came not to condemn but to allow men to live life to the fullest.' I mean, just think about it! God created the universe from nothing. God created human nature. He took on human nature just to be with us and show us how to live life! Does it not make sense that his commandments and life-style would make us happy? It really is not that surprising if you stop and think about it."

I was blown away by his answer. But I had one more nagging question.

"That is all amazing, but if that is true, why is it so hard to live out what God wants for us? He could have made it so much easier for us to be happy."

Jake stroked his chin hair as he thought, and eventually said, "Well, there are three answers to that. First off, God originally did make it easy for us, but our ancestors disobeyed and gave us concupiscence. Original sin makes it so difficult for us to live lives of virtue. But second, Christ entered human nature and he lived a life of struggles and suffering. God himself endured hardship here on earth; why should we expect anything different? And third, he gave us a path to make resisting sin easier. We have sacramentals such as the Rosary and the seven sacraments. If you receive the sacraments often, then you will receive the grace to resist the sins you are finding difficult to give up. It is not God's fault that we choose sin or find virtue difficult to attain. The grace God has for us is always sufficient against our temptations."

After this conversation, I arranged to visit him at Franciscan University during the upcoming spring semester. When I went back home, I initially returned to Mass, started reading spiritual books, and attempted to pray daily. This initial resurgence in the Faith faded as I continued to hang out with my friends and engage in impure relationships. I knew what I was doing was wrong and would not make me happy. And yet I continued to do it, which only made my anxiety and self-doubt increase even more than it was before I talked with Jake. I could not wait for my visit to Franciscan University; I needed to receive more answers to my questions and find the courage to quit the lifestyle I was stuck in.

The visit inevitably came, and it was everything I thought it would be and more. After Jake picked me up from the airport and introduced me to a few of his friends, one of the first things we did was pray in his dorm chapel. Upon entering the chapel, I lazily genuflected and took a seat in one of the chairs. My cousin Jake, however, fell to his knees and bowed his face to the floor in reverence. I was profoundly confused but also impressed by this gesture. I had never seen anyone show such respect for the Eucharist; I had never seen anyone truly treat the Sacrament for what the Church taught that it was: God.

While we were praying, a group of students came in and whispered to Jake and me that they had to clear the chapel of its chairs since their household (essentially a Catholic version of fraternities) and their visitors were going to pray the Rosary. Jake asked me if I wanted to stay and pray the Rosary with this group, and I expressed interest. I could not remember the last time I had prayed a whole Rosary, and thus I had no idea what all the prayers were, but I was intrigued to see what would happen. Men and women began to enter the chapel, and they all displayed the same level of reverence for the Eucharist present in the tabernacle that Jake had. These were young adults, students from freshmen to seniors, who were not embarrassed to demonstrate their faith boldly.

The Rosary began with songs that I had never heard before, which I later found out were from Hillsong United. I looked around, and the young men and women around me were extending their hands toward the tabernacle, seemingly giving their all to Christ. I was bewildered; I could not manage to focus on praying due to the display of faith that was taking place all around me. The scriptural Rosary was said by the members of the household, pausing between each bead to read a verse from Scripture that pertained to the mystery of the Rosary we were meditating. The Rosary ended with the singing of the *Salve Regina*, which was one of the most beautiful prayers I had ever had the pleasure to participate in.

After the prayers had ceased, Jake turned to me and asked if I was ready to leave. I slowly nodded my head, amazed at what I had just witnessed. The rest of the week did not disappoint either: every conversation I had with Jake and his friends was focused on what was holy, true, good, and beautiful. My sides hurt from laughter, my brain was stimulated from intellectual conversations, and my soul was cleansed after confession and attending daily Mass. I was even blessed to receive the opportunity to attend one of Jake's classes, which just so happened to be taught by the man who wrote the book I was reading, Patrick Madrid.

While I did not necessarily have true faith yet, I promised myself that I would amend my life as I went back home. I called off the promiscuous "hanging out" I was participating in with a girl from back home, I attended non-obligatory days for Mass, and I began listening to Christian music and reading spiritual books. But without any community and support, my largely emotional resurgence in the Faith collapsed. In my mind, I was still a practicing Catholic since I started to make compromises. I kept drinking and smoking, but I no longer sought to be promiscuous outside of committed relationships. I broke Catholic moral teaching on chastity with my girlfriend, but I strove to avoid pornography. In my mind, these compromises balanced out my faith and justified my sins. Of course, I would inevitably break those compromises when the temptations were too prevalent, but I justified those to myself as well, which was a monumental mistake.

Finally, my senior year came. This would be the year that I decided which college I would attend, and I had begun doubting whether I truly wanted to attend Franciscan University. Sure, I loved visiting there two years ago, but I was different now. I wanted to play football and Franciscan did not have a football program, and that was how it was going to be. I had still applied to Franciscan since I promised Jake and his friends that I would, but I did not intend on attending the university. God had other plans, however. During my last year of football, playing as the starting middle linebacker on an undefeated team, I got mono. I was sidelined for the rest of the season and watched as my team lost its first game in the semi-finals, losing 52-51 in overtime. I cried like I had never cried before. I knew that if I were playing, the result of the game would have been different, I raged against God in anger and frustration as the visiting team celebrated on our home field.

The rest of my senior year was extraordinarily dark. I entered a relationship with a girl, completely ignoring the Church's teaching on chastity. I began indulging in all the carnal pleasures I had tried to turn away from. I did anything in my power to make God feel how I had felt when I had (from my perspective) unjustly received mono. I had committed myself to living a life against order, to challenge laws and push the envelope whenever I could. It was not until I got into trouble with the law that I began to wake up from my dark path. I knew I was handling my suffering from football entirely inappropriately and that I had made an idol out of this sport and of myself playing it. I was unwilling to leave the relationship that I was in, but I committed myself to attending Franciscan University. I saw how miserable I was making myself by entirely denying God, and I wanted to try and make sense of the suffering I had endured. Merely waving my fist at the sky and pretending that my suffering was pointless and nihilistic solved nothing. I needed to confront my cross and try and find meaning.

I attended Franciscan in the fall and instantly met the people who would change my life forever. My roommate, Ryan, would become my best friend, my dorm neighbor, Sebastian, would become one of my closest friends, and many friends both male and female (including my fiancée!) I would meet through the household known as the Disciples. It was not until later that I realized the Disciples were the same household I had prayed the Rosary with when I visited Jake. Eventually, due to all these gifts from God, my high school relationship ended with a breakup, albeit she was the one to breakup with me. While initially very painful, this too was a grace from God.

After a long and confusing summer, desiring to see my ex-girlfriend again, I still had not accepted the fact that I needed to begin living out the Faith. I returned to school to begin my sophomore year, still struggling to live out the Faith and no longer having any excuses not to. In a moment of spiritual dryness, I had decided to attend a Festival of Praise (FOP) at Franciscan, which was a celebration of the Faith through praise and worship music.

I had always been skeptical of these events; I was not a very charismatic person when it came to prayer. Perhaps I have always been a traditionalist on the inside and just did not realize it. I felt very isolated and cutoff from God, however, and so I was desperate, willing to turn anywhere to feel a connection to him.

While at the FOP, the stereotypical songs and worship experiences occurred. I actively participated and admittedly had a good time. Yet, it was not the loud music, flashing lights, or charismatic prayer that made me reconnect with God. It was the exposure of the Eucharist in silent and prayerful adoration. In the middle of the conference, a priest walked through the crowd carrying the Eucharist in a monstrance. It was in this moment that everything came together: I was looking at Jesus Christ, the God-man who had died for my sins, established the Catholic Church, and humbled himself in the appearance of bread and wine just to be with his creation. Silently, I allowed tears to fall from my face, tears of joy and contentment rather than anger, frustration, confusion, or resentment. I finally understood that I was a Roman Catholic, and I needed to follow all the teachings of the Faith by amending my life.

I had finally bitten the bullet and accepted that I was a Catholic and that I needed to fulfill my identity by adhering to the moral dictates of Mother Church. When you first meet someone special or you are newlywed, that person can do no wrong in your eyes. She appears to be the most amazing person in the world. I was in the honeymoon phase of conversion, and everything and anything about Catholicism grabbed my attention and interest. This was the twist I promised at the beginning of this tale, the typical witness story ends with a happily ever after once the person joins the Catholic Church. But that is *not* the end of the story. It is crucial to understand the honeymoon phase in order to understand why there is a growing traditional Catholic movement.

While I had always been put off by praise and worship music in the liturgy, I began to attend FOPs more regularly and began participating in Steubenville Masses. Nothing captures the honeymoon phase of the Faith more than a Steubenville Mass. If you have ever attended one, then you know precisely what I mean by that. When I first attended a Steubenville Mass with my cousin Jake, I had felt like I had entered an authentic Broadway musical, but I was the only one who did not know the words. While my former church's music sounded like a cheap Broadway knockoff, Steubenville Masses were the real deal—it appeared that everyone at the campus was musically gifted.

On top of my enthusiasm for an admittedly false version of active participation and entertainment during Mass, I had taken an interest in reading the works of Pope John Paul II and Pope Benedict XVI and other modern Catholic apologists. I read *Love and Responsibility*, I bought *Introduction to Christianity*, and devoured anything and everything written by Tim Staples. *Catholic Answers* became my go-to for every answer or question of the Faith. Any perspective or opinion of the Faith I gained came from these three sources: *Catholic Answers*, Pope John Paul II, and Pope Benedict XVI. No offense to these three resources, but they are clearly not the totality of the Faith. I had left the fullness of the Catholic intellectual tradition largely undiscovered during this period, so I was still very ignorant on a lot of teachings despite my unbounded confidence in my apologetic abilities.

This began to change during the spring semester of my sophomore year when I attended the sister campus in Gaming, Austria. The students, teachers, countries, and academic curriculum I encountered during this program served as the foundation for the knowledge you will read in the following pages. I would like to provide a walk-through for how I was introduced to this material. I fell in love with philosophy, culture, religion, theology, politics, and virtue through the presentation of the curriculum by my teachers. While I was studying these courses and reading some of the greatest works of literature ever written, I was also exploring Europe and experiencing the culture of Western civilization firsthand. By studying in Austria, I learned the rational roots of the Catholic faith as well as the arguments against atheism and secularism in a manner which had never been presented to me before. All the modern debates about God, morality, and the nature of reality had all been grappled with thousands of years ago by the ancient Greeks, the Church Fathers, and the medieval Scholastics.

It seemed as if nothing could shake me from my honeymoon phase; the more I read about the Church, the more enthralled I became with her. But just as with any human relationship, my infatuation started to fade. After Austria, I felt God pull away from me, asking me to seek him further. I was getting stimulated by reading the Church's intellectual tradition, such as saints Augustine and Aquinas, but my prayer life was not getting the same level of attention as my academic endeavors. I kept attending FOPs, charismatic prayer services, and actively participating at Mass but to no avail. God did not come rushing back into my life like he did when I reverted. If the Church's intellectual tradition was stimulating, complex, and dense, then surely its liturgical tradition must also be just as gripping. I was opening myself up to the Lord, yet I felt empty and experienced no emotional or spiritual comfort from prayer. What was I missing?

I told my friends about what I was experiencing, and thankfully, they gave me helpful advice. One friend, who used to be a Protestant, instructed me by stating that God was pulling himself away so that I would seek him out in deeper ways. I was confused but comforted by his words and continued to listen intently. He described how I needed to start developing an *interior prayer life* rather than merely exteriorly praising and worshiping God. He explained how I needed to confront God through meditation and fasting. This sounded difficult and, frankly, too strict and traditionalist; however, he managed to connect these practices with Saint Francis and Saint Clare and explained that it was through these devotions that they managed to experience ongoing conversion. He told the story of how Saint Francis would spend hours in front of the Eucharist in silent meditation and prayer, sometimes devoting his whole night in front of an exposed Host, and then spend the day preaching.

Saint Francis had a profound and mature relationship with God, but it did not come merely from listening to the Hillsong United song *Oceans* on a guitar and waving his hands around. He experienced ongoing conversion through discipline and penance. I suddenly began to contemplate the nature of the Novus Ordo Masses I had been exposed to and my dependency on external participation in order to worship God. The saints grew closer to God through silence, contemplation, adoration, reverence, and discipline. Yet, almost all the acts of worship at the Steubenville Masses were the exact opposite: loud, compulsive, indifferent, at times irreverent, and undisciplined. While I initially desired to grow closer to God through the same methods I saw my fellow university students utilizing, I eventually began skipping those events in favor of traditional devotions and practices to attain a stronger prayer life.

Thankfully for me, Steubenville also offered plenty of experiences to develop traditional devotions. Some of these traditional devotions included signing up for a weekly Holy Hour, praying the Rosary daily, wearing the brown scapular, signing up for service at a soup kitchen, taking Lent seriously with strict fasting, offering up bread and water fasts, and finding novenas and consecrations to pray. These traditional devotions brought an incredible amount of spiritual fruit into my life: I went from spiritual dryness to an oasis. Yet, there was still something missing in my religious journey. I was able to experience reverence, discipline, and penance in every aspect of my life except for the one that was the most important: the Holy Mass. My thoughts as a seventh-grade boy came flooding back to me; I re-discovered that the liturgy was overly emotional, undisciplined, and comfortable but nearly every other aspect of my life was the opposite. The monumental and important difference between now and then was that instead of comparing the discipline and structure of football practice with the liturgy, I was now comparing my prayer life with the liturgy. There had to be an answer to the disconnect between the traditional prayer devotions I was embracing and the average Novus Ordo liturgy.

I eventually discovered the liturgy that matched the traditional prayer devotions: the Traditional Latin Mass. There were so many people, occurrences, and conversations that led to my discovery of the Mass of the ages, but to tell you all of these would fill a whole book. To condense my thoughts, I will present a three-pronged explanation as to why the Traditional Latin Mass matches the necessary requirements for a deeper relationship with God: First, we will discuss the notion of *lex orandi, lex credendi, lex vivendi*. Then we will observe the difference between theocentric and anthropocentric liturgies. And finally, we will discuss the comparison between the contemplative interior participation of the Latin Mass and the non-contemplative external participation of the Novus Ordo.

Lex orandi, lex credendi, lex vivendi is a Latin phrase meaning "as we pray, so we believe, so we live." This phrase is first found in the writings of Prosper of Aquitaine (390–455), who argued that the prayers and structure of the liturgy were apostolic in origin and therefore a source for discovering the true doctrines of the Church.[1] So, hypothetically, if we were to observe how modern

---

[1]   See *Catechism of the Catholic Church*, no. 1124.

Catholics lived, we could discover what they believed and therefore a significant amount about how they worshiped. All one must do is reread the introduction of this book to discover that both what Catholics believe and how they act are extremely divorced from the Church's faith and morals. If what modern Catholics believe (*credendi*) and how they live (*vivendi*) are divorced from the Faith, it is not farfetched to make the conclusion that there might be something wrong with how the average Catholic is worshiping (*orandi*).

It can be concluded that from the time of the ancient Church to the modern Catechism, the principle of *lex orandi, lex vivendi* has been held as a valid principle. If how we worship effects how we live and there is something wrong with the way modern Catholics worship, what is the problem with modern worship that is causing a lack of faith? To answer this question, we will now compare theocentric and anthropocentric liturgies. A theocentric liturgy is focused on God-centered prayer, a liturgy that places the Sacrifice of Christ as its center and focal point. An anthropocentric liturgy is focused on the people in attendance, community, and the personal experiences of those who are in attendance. Pope Benedict XVI gave us the qualifications for what constitutes an anthropocentric liturgy: "The liturgical reform, in its concrete realization, has distanced itself even more from its origin. The result has not been a reanimation, but *devastation*. In place of the liturgy, fruit of a continual development, they have placed a *fabricated liturgy*. They have deserted a vital process of growth and becoming in order to substitute a fabrication. They did not

want to continue the development, the organic matur-
ing of something living through the centuries, and they
replaced it, in the manner of technical production, by a
fabrication, a *banal product of the moment*."[2]

These are harsh words from a post-conciliar pope, but
he is exactly right. The liturgical reform sacrificed entering the transcendent realm of heaven for "a banal product
of the moment." He explained better than I ever could
why I was not attracted to the liturgy once I had reached
my adolescent years. Once I had grown older, I could tell
that something was missing in my local parish's Mass
due to the shallowness of the liturgy. Unfortunately,
this phenomenon is not unique to my small-town New
Hampshire parish but is a global epidemic.

It does not matter how talented or good hearted the
contemporary music ministry at your local parish is, or
how reverent your extraordinary Eucharistic ministers
are, they will never be able to escape the fact that they are
contemporary and a part of the *anthropocentric* additions
to the liturgy.[3] Most Novus Ordo Masses are oriented
toward the people, and the orientation of these Masses
have a direct impact on the rest of the liturgy. The orientation of the liturgy leads to the anthropocentric
additions discussed above. This is due to the symbolism
and subconscious impact of having the priest face the

---

[2]   Joseph Ratzinger, *Revue Theologisches*, Vol. 20, Feb. 1990, pp.
        103–4, emphasis mine.
[3]   Athanasius Schneider and Diane Montagna, *Christus Vin-
        cit: Christ's Triumph Over the Darkness of the Age* (Brooklyn:
        Angelico Press, 2019), p. 228.

congregation when he prays instead of Christ the King in the tabernacle.

Another important feature of the traditional Mass that the Novus Ordo lacks is *silence*. This is not to say that sacred music does not play an important role in the liturgy, far from it, but sacred music is not the type of noise I am talking about that disrupts silence. I am discussing the nature of the Novus Ordo in regards to the Mass responses, the reading of the canon in an overtly audible voice, and the almost constant interruption of silence by either the priest or the laity to ensure that the congregation is not losing interest or lacking in participation. This overemphasis on ensuring that no one is left behind or feels as if they cannot participate causes the exact problem that the implementation of the Novus Ordo was trying to avoid: it makes it easier for individuals to zone out due to familiarity. On the other hand, the traditional Mass will not stop to make sure everyone is on the same page; it drives the point home that the liturgy is about offering the Holy Sacrifice to *God* on your behalf; it's not about *you*.

If you have ever desired a liturgy that matches your personal devotions for reverence and discipline, if you have ever desired for your worship to be more akin to heaven on earth and less like a man-centered Broadway musical note, and if you have ever desired to worship Christ as he desires to be worshiped rather than a form of worship that is directed and focused on humanity, *then attend the Traditional Latin Mass*. But if you cannot access a traditional parish, then begin slowly implementing traditional devotions at your Novus Ordo parish. Start by suggesting to your priest to say Masses *ad orientem* rather than *versus populum* or ask if he would consider bringing back the communion-plate (the plate for receiving Communion at the Mass), discuss altering the music at Mass to reflect the reality of the liturgy as a sacrifice. If everyone reading this chapter writes two to three letters to their local bishop encouraging the return of traditional devotions in the liturgy, we could start a counter-revolution against anthropocentrism and slowly start returning the liturgy to its rightful theocentric orientation. This is the story of my conversion from a cafeteria Catholic to a Novus Ordo active participant and finally to a Traditional Latin Mass attendant. I have taken the tradpill. Will you?

CONCLUSION

THERE HAVE been almost innumerable experiences of average Catholics becoming tradpilled. Some are joyful occasions, others humorous, and still others tragic. Dr. Taylor Marshall described his tradpill moment in his podcast with Timothy Gordon; it occurred when he went to receive Holy Communion after converting from Anglicanism to Catholicism. But instead of using an altar rail, a communion-plate, and receiving from a priest (as done in the Anglican Church), he was receiving Communion from a layperson wearing a Grover t-shirt. Yes, Grover from *Sesame Street*. It was in that moment that Dr. Marshall no longer wanted to attend the Novus Ordo Mass, and he began to seek out a more traditional parish.

My tradpill moment was not as lighthearted. I teach at a Catholic school in Manchester, New Hampshire. Every day, we attend Mass at the parish that is directly next to our school, which was a source of peace for me before starting the school day. One day before Mass, however, I was doing more research into the Novus Ordo, and I stumbled upon an article written by a traditionalist.[1] In the article, the author described how the

---

[1] To this day, I cannot find that article. But a similar article can be found at *The Remnant* newspaper. Yáñez, Miguel Ángel, "Communion in the Hand: The Floor Is Stained with His Blood," *The Remnant*, March 30, 2016, https://remnantnews

communion-plate had been diabolically abandoned after the Second Vatican Council, and now particles of the Sacred Host are carelessly allowed to fall to the floor. I rolled my eyes as I read this, but the author wrote a message anticipating skepticism from Novus Ordo attending Catholics. The author challenged his Novus Ordo readers to look down at the floor when they go up to receive Communion and see if they can find any particles or fragments of the Host.

I was perplexed. It was a very simple idea, and yet it was also something that I never would have noticed unless instructed to search for it. I thought to myself how easy it would be to disprove the article, so I confidently clicked the exit button on the browser and began to start my day. During Mass, I had almost forgotten about the article until it was the time to receive Communion. The idea entered my head again as I was walking up to receive, so I said a prayer that I may receive Communion worthily and in an undistracted manner. But I could not help but open my eyes before receiving to check the floor. To my horror, I saw pieces of white flakes on the floor by the priest's foot. I received Communion and was utterly scandalized by what I had just seen.

For the rest of Mass, I began to pray, asking the Lord for forgiveness if I had stepped on him and for never even considering the amount of abuse that takes place to his precious body without a communion-plate. When the Mass had ended, I waited for the students to clear out. Once

---

paper.com/web/index.php/articles/item/2399-communion-in-the-hand-the-floor-is-stained-with-his-blood.

they were gone, I carefully stepped over to the area where I had seen the fragments. They were still roughly in the same spot, albeit slightly scattered from where they were previously. I began audibly praying the Hail Mary while I picked up the fragments and placed them into my hand.

While I was doing this, a woman from the parish walked up to me and asked me what I was doing. I showed her the fragments of what I believed to be the Host. She took one, placed a fragment on her tongue, and then said, "It must be a cracker! It tastes sweet."

I responded, "So does the Host; the Host tastes sweet and has the accidents of a cracker, or host."

She shook her head and told me that I was worrying too much. I received the fragments on the tongue, horrified by the events that transpired. This event affected me more than any of the intellectual arguments, prophecies, visions, or heresies I encountered in my research of the traditionalist movement. But in this moment, all those resources were enhanced and given extreme clarity. The words of Our Lady of Good Success echoed in my head: "*My Most Holy Son will see Himself cast upon the ground and trampled upon by filthy feet.*"[2] Later on, I read a quote from Bishop Athanasius Schneider that confirmed this uncomfortable and horrific tragedy: "There is the grievous fact of the loss of Eucharistic fragments because of Communion in the hand. No one can deny this. Fragments of the consecrated host fall to the floor and are subsequently crushed by feet.

---

[2]   Manuel Sousa Pereira, "The Admirable Life of Mother Mariana Volume I," *Tradition in Action Inc*, 2005.

This is horrible! Our God is trampled on in our churches! No one can deny it. This is happening on a large scale."[3]

I was officially tradpilled.

Now, this tragedy might not be enough to tradpill *you*, however. This was a personal experience that might not affect the average reader; hopefully, whoever is reading this does not attend a parish where the Eucharist is left open to abuse! If my personal experience, the experiences from the other authors above, and their arguments are not enough to convince you of embracing tradition, then the only things that can are prayer and attending a traditional Mass for yourself. More than any story or argument, prayer and the traditional Mass can demonstrate the reality of the Church's beauty, goodness, and truth found in her traditional devotions. Attending the Latin Mass for the first three times can be very difficult and different, but it is just like Pope Benedict XVI said, "The Extraordinary Form is difficult in the way that anything that's rewarding is difficult, like classical music when what we know is mainly popular music."[4]

What can be done to help bring traditional devotions and liturgy back? As with any movement, it's important for traditionalists to understand the rights they have at their disposal. The Church grants the laity a variety of rights, and these rights which often relate to the liturgy. Consider these four rights:

3   Athanasius Schneider and Diane Montagna, *Christus Vincit: Christ's Triumph Over the Darkness of the Age* (Brooklyn: Angelico Press, 2019), p. 230.

4   Nicholas Frankovich, "It's Extraordinary," *First Things*, September 26, 2013.

1. *"The faithful have a right to a true Liturgy.* . . . Undue experimentation, changes and creativity bewilder the faithful. The use of unauthorized texts means a loss of the necessary connection between the *lex orandi* and the *lex credendi*. The Second Vatican Council's admonition in this regard must be remembered: 'No person, even if he be a priest, may add, remove or change anything in the Liturgy on his own authority'" (*General Instruction of the Roman Missal*).

2. "Anyone who takes advantage of the reform to indulge in arbitrary experiments is wasting energy and offending the ecclesial sense" (Paul VI, address of August 22, 1973: *L'Osservatore Romano*, August 23, 1973).

3. "The parish priest is to take care that the blessed Eucharist is the center of the parish assembly of the faithful. He is to strive to ensure that the faithful are nourished by *the devout celebration of the sacraments*, and in particular that they *frequently* approach the sacraments of the blessed Eucharist *and penance*. He is to strive to lead them to prayer, including prayer in their families, and to take a live and active part in the sacred liturgy. Under the authority of the diocesan Bishop, the parish priest must direct this liturgy in his own parish, *and he is bound to be on guard against abuses*" (Canon 528 ß2).

4. *Dominicae Cenae* and the *General Instruction for the Roman Missal* guarantee the Faithful the right to receive on the tongue at whatever parish they attend, with no exceptions.

Take advantage of these rights, point out to your direct

superiors that they have an obligation to provide to you as a Catholic the traditions of our Faith. If you cannot influence your parish priest to implement the traditions of the Church, then try to find another more reverent parish. There is a wonderful app for smartphones known as I-Mass, which was created by the Priestly Fraternity of St. Peter (FSSP). It will direct you to all their parishes worldwide, as well as any diocesan or Institute of Christ the King Sovereign Priest (ICKSP) parishes that offer the traditional Mass.

And if you cannot find a parish that offers a more reverent liturgy, you can start by implementing traditional devotions in your life. Pray a Rosary daily, wear a scapular, go to confession frequently, receive Communion on your tongue while kneeling, start practicing the traditional forms of fasting and meditation, and encourage your friends and family to join you. If you are a woman, start wearing a veil to Mass, and if you are a man, start wearing suits to make yourself look presentable. If you are a priest and you do not know how to say the traditional Mass and are willing to learn, there are plenty of workshops and conferences that can assist you. There may be a situation in which you are a priest and cannot learn or say the traditional Mass, and if that is the case, then begin to implement beautiful architecture, music, and devotions into your Novus Ordo liturgies.

You might not think that your private implementation of traditional devotions will make a difference in the world, but in moments of doubt, you should remember the example of Saint Thérèse of Lisieux. There is a story about the Little Flower that has always struck me, but I have no proof it is a true story. She would pray not by asking God for specific intentions but by merely placing radical trust in the Lord. She would start her prayer sessions by stating (not an exact quote), "I ask you, God, to shed your grace where it is most needed in the Church, in the world, in the lives of my loved ones, and my own life." She prayed this way every day, and one day, a cardinal came and visited her cloister. He was permitted to meet the sisters of the convent, and when he saw Saint Thérèse, he got excited and exclaimed, "You! You are the one who has been praying for me!"

The saint was very confused, but the cardinal continued to explain that in a dream, she was shown to him and a voice declared, "She is the reason you have become a cardinal." Without even realizing it, the Little Flower had assisted a man to one of the highest positions of our Church merely by doing a simple daily devotion that no one knew about except for her and God. Imagine the graces you can bring into this world by starting personal prayer devotions, evangelizing through tradition, and calling on your Catholic leaders to do the same.

It is with this hopeful pondering that I will conclude this anthology. Why are younger generations embracing traditional Catholicism? Because the traditions of the Church will *never die*. The tradition of Holy Mother Church is analogous to how Saint Augustine described God: "ever ancient, ever new." Traditional Catholicism is not a fad. It is not a phase. Tradition is the past, present, and future of Holy Mother Church.

Viva Christo Rey!

—Kenneth Alexander